Perfect English
Farmhouse

Perfect English
Farmhouse

Ros Byam Shaw

with photography by JAN BALDWIN

RYLAND PETERS & SMALL
LONDON • NEW YORK

This book is dedicated to Lydia

Designer Paul Tilby

Editor Annabel Morgan

Location research Ros Byam Shaw
& Jess Walton

Production Gordana Simakovic

Art director Leslie Harrington

Editorial director Julia Charles

First published in 2012.
This revised edition published in 2017
by Ryland Peters & Small
20–21 Jockey's Fields,
London WC1R 4BW
and
341 East 116th Street
New York, NY 10029
www.rylandpeters.com

10 9 8 7 6 5 4 3 2

ISBN: 978-1-84975-878-9

Library of Congress Cataloging-in-
Publication Data has been applied for.

A CIP record for this book is available
from the British Library.

Printed and bound in China

CONTENTS

INTRODUCTION

The English countryside is studded with farms; clusters of buildings holding together the landscape like buttons in a mattress. Many are still working farms, their yards stained with dung, their sheds crammed with the machinery of modern agriculture. But as the size of a workable farm has continued to grow, an increasing number of farmhouses have been sold off to make homes for people whose livelihoods are less closely connected with the land that surrounds them.

Writing a book about houses and the way their owners occupy them is always an intriguing prospect. Farmhouses promised to be a particularly rich seam of interest, varying in size as they do from modest cottages to the spacious abodes of wealthy yeoman, enfolded by the fields and pasture that supported them. After my initial disappointment that none of the farmhouses were part of traditional working farms, this has proved to be one of the most enterprising and creative groups of owners I have been lucky enough to meet.

Whilst not working farms, most of these farmhouses are still places of work. Often they have been bought complete with outbuildings, and with a few acres of land. But instead

of milking, or processing corn or shearing sheep, the people who live in them are making things, selling things, designing things or sharing the beauty of their architecture and surrounding countryside with paying guests. Some are doing more than one of the above.

Among them are a sculptor, a potter, a leather worker and a textile designer, all with workshops in converted barns, and another textile designer with a studio in a spare bedroom plus an office in the attic. There is a dealer in old master paintings, and there are two other owners who have turned barns into antiques shops. There are holiday cottages and studios in piggeries, stables and cowsheds. There is a guest annexe in a stable, and an office in a granary. Even the remains of more modern farm buildings have been put to use. William Peers has built a huge greenhouse on the footings of one, while Ursula and Toby Falconer have transformed the remains of a particularly ugly specimen into a walled garden.

As for the land, it is being put to equally productive use, with vegetable gardens, orchards and beehives. Many owners keep chickens, but there are also pigs, sheep, quail, geese and a small herd of Charolais cattle. Other means of making the land pay its way include campsites, yurts and a 'wild wood' used as a location for film and photography. Some houses have their own water supply, nearly all are online, and most of the businesses being run from these sometimes quite isolated places are made possible by access to the internet.

OPPOSITE Off the living room in Doris Urquhart and Christopher Richardson's Suffolk farmhouse is a room once used as a dairy. ABOVE LEFT The shelves of Alison Hill's pantry are lined with preserving jars. ABOVE CENTRE Bella Pringle's kitchen is an extension built against the back of the original farmhouse, while Holly Keeling has turned the piggery at the back of her farmhouse, ABOVE RIGHT, into a studio.

ABOVE The curtains at Eva Johnson's kitchen windows are made from antique linen tea towels, as are the cushions on the stools. The window overlooks a cobbled courtyard on the other side of which is a game larder.

Only one farmhouse in the book has retained its original acreage. This is Botelet in Cornwall, and its story is a reflection of the changes in agriculture that have taken place in the space of just four generations. Botelet has been in the same family since 1860. When Thomas Tamblyn bought it from the Trelawny estate at the beginning of the 20th century, having lived and worked there as a tenant, the land produced enough income to support his family. Hay, straw and grain were harvested in summer to feed the cattle and sheep through winter when bullocks were fattened off in the barns and sold one at a time to local butchers. Horses did all the heavy work instead of tractors, and there were no telephone, electricity or fuel bills.

Thomas's son Cyrus saw the introduction of tractors, and of electricity, which finally came to the farm to power the corn drier. Electricity had to be paid for, so production was increased. Artificial fertilizers were introduced and some of

the hedges taken out to make bigger fields. Processed cattle feed was bought to supplement food grown on the farm, and a combine harvester speeded up the grain harvest. A pump was installed to take water to animals in fields without streams.

In the early 1960s, Cyrus's son David started building a herd of Charolais cattle for beef. More fields were seeded out to grass, and hay and silage were harvested. Some grain was grown, and also green crops for the sheep. It was hard work for low pay, and it was dangerous; David was kicked in the face by a cow, the floor of a barn collapsed and both David and his son Richard narrowly missed being buried alive in an avalanche of grain. In the 1980s, David decided to semi-retire. The Charolais herd and the sheep were sold, and all the fields were seeded to grass and let to neighbouring farmers.

Ten years ago, Botelet joined the Countryside Stewardship Scheme, with its emphasis on conservation, restoring old hedges, creating wildlife habitats, keeping production low and abandoning artificial fertilizers and sprays. The land is now used for grazing cattle and sheep between April and October, and is allowed to rest for the winter months. As a result, many wild flowers and rare birds have returned to the fields. Richard and David's care is now the land itself, rather than animals and crops. David carries a chair around his fields, sitting to prise out the staples from wooden fence posts so that the wire stock fencing can be replaced, while the old is rolled up to keep for future repairs. Among other works of restoration and conservation, Richard is rebuilding a rare, medieval Cornish 'wide wall' at the back of the farmhouse, which historians think may have originally been used as a viewing platform for games of bowls.

While agribusiness encourages farming on an ever bigger scale, there is an opposite move by individuals towards small-scale animal husbandry and home-grown produce, 'farming of the Marie Antoinette variety,' as one owner puts it. Inevitably, the selection of country dwellers in this book is very far from representative, but it is inspiring. And, even on a small scale, it is good to know that wild flowers and rare birds are ready to return to our countryside when the conditions are right for them.

OPPOSITE A stable door in the entrance hall of William Peers and Sophie Poklewski-Koziell's Cornish farmhouse incorporates a window allowing extra light into the room. The hats on sticks are arranged in a wicker basket like enormous flowers in a giant vase. The walls are built of cob, and the floor tiles were made by William using local clay.

Behold the sound oak table's massy frame
Bestride the kitchen floor! the careful dame
And gen'rous host invite their friends around,
While all that cleared the crop, or tilled the ground,
Are guests by right of custom

ROBERT BLOOMFIELD (1766–1823)

ORGANIC
FARMHOUSE

THE WORD 'ORGANIC' HAS BECOME ONE OF THOSE FASHIONABLE TAGS THAT ATTACHES TO EVERYTHING FROM T-SHIRTS TO BREAD. WE HOPE AND TRUST THAT THESE ARE PRODUCTS GROWN OR NURTURED MORE NATURALLY THAN THEIR NON-ORGANIC EQUIVALENTS, USING FEWER HARMFUL PESTICIDES AND CHEMICAL INTERVENTIONS. THE FARMHOUSES IN THIS CHAPTER ARE NOT ORGANIC IN THIS SENSE OF THE WORD, ALTHOUGH THE CHICKENS KEPT AND THE LETTUCES GROWN BY THEIR OWNERS ALMOST CERTAINLY ARE. THIS IS ORGANIC AS A STYLE OF DECORATING — EARTHY, RUSTIC, SIMPLE. AND AS WHOLESOME AND DELICIOUS AS A HOME-MADE LOAF.

OPPOSITE In the kitchen, the carver chair and the table were made by William's father, Robin Peers, and the two primitive ladder-back chairs were made by William. The terracotta floor tiles are also home-made; William dug the clay for them locally, and even built the kiln, which he tended for two days and two nights – an enterprise he describes as 'fringing on insanity'.

RIGHT The larger of the barns is a workshop where William carves sculptures from blocks of marble.

FAR RIGHT The stone barn adjoining the house has been converted to make an office.

BELOW The house is built from cob and was dilapidated and 'completely unloved' when they first saw it.

CARVING A HOME

'We shape our buildings, and afterwards they shape us,' said Winston Churchill, arguing for the reconstruction of the old House of Commons, which had been destroyed in the blitz. It's a quote that sculptor William Peers finds especially appealing. He and his wife Sophie Poklewski Koziell have shaped the building they inhabit more comprehensively than most. They have moulded cob (a mixture of clay and straw) to mend its walls, sawn and planed wood to make its floors, doors and stairs, and dug and mixed the clay for its floor tiles – literally shaping the rooms with their own hands. As for how the house has shaped them, William simply smiles and shrugs. But you only have to spend a day in their thoughtful, hospitable and creative company to sense the answer.

The couple first came to Cornwall in the late 1990s and rented a cottage. William already knew the area and Sophie felt at home in the landscape, which reminded her of County Kildare, where she spent her childhood.

They viewed the house on the strength of an 'awful picture' in an estate agent's office, and instantly fell for it. Part of the attraction was the clutch of farm buildings gathered closely around the house – barns and animal sheds that offered the space William needs for his work as a sculptor, teasing sensual shape and texture from unwieldy slabs of marble. They were also attracted by its untouched, unspoilt condition – the very thing that had deterred less intrepid buyers.

Built of cob with stone foundations beneath an undulating roof of large, irregular slates, the house has the rooted look of a structure crafted from the landscape it occupies. With no garden to separate it from surrounding meadows, it seems to hug the slope of land that dips down to the banks of the River Tamar. It is hard to say how old it is. 'It is quite an impoverished building,' says William. 'There is nothing of any architectural stature or expense. The smartest thing in the whole house is the granite fireplace in our bedroom. I don't think the farmers who lived here can ever have made any money.'

Lack of spare cash had preserved the interior. Far from having been stripped back and polished to the point of bland nonentity, as is the fate of so many 'restored' old houses, it had accreted layers beneath

ABOVE LEFT William's father, an agricultural engineer, built two new oak staircases for the house, including this one that leads up from the living room. William made the log basket, and the wide oak floorboards were cut from Shropshire oak given to William and Sophie as a wedding present.

ABOVE Sophie says she always wanted donkeys, and always wanted to play the trumpet. Now she has both, and says that the donkeys, Amir and Hassan, join in by braying when she strikes up a tune.

FAR LEFT There are fresh eggs for breakfast, thanks to the hens that cluck in the garden.

OPPOSITE The barn next to the house has been converted into an office and guest accommodation. The oak-framed sofas on castors, made to William and Sophie's own design, can be wheeled together to make a double bed. Wide planks cut from an ancient oak tree felled locally are seasoning in the barn and will be laid as flooring.

ABOVE Slate shelves line the larder, stacked with jars of wholesome home-made jams and chutneys, as well as slightly more frivolous lollipops.

OPPOSITE The cat has just had kittens and sleeps on a sheepskin rug next to the warmth of the Aga. Like so much in the house, the kitchen units are home-made, as is the stone draining board, beautifully carved with fern-shaped runnels by William.

which the original house remained intact, if somewhat dilapidated. Beams had been boxed in, walls and ceilings straightened up, fireplaces covered. 'When we started removing the later additions,' says William, 'all the rooms were several feet bigger than they had been.'

Most of the original woodwork was irreparable. A welcome wedding present from William's father Robin was Shropshire oak, which they seasoned and used to make beautiful wide floorboards both upstairs and down. An agricultural engineer who designed the first successful raspberry picking machine, Robin Peers

TOP LEFT William has used local materials wherever possible, such as the Cornish slate behind the butler's sink in the entrance hall – a convenient place to wash the home-grown vegetables picked from raised beds in the greenhouse, which he built on the footings of another barn.

ABOVE In the same room, the fireplace alcove makes useful storage for hats, baskets and a feather duster.

ABOVE The bathtub was found abandoned in a neighbouring farmyard, while the lavatory cistern has a home-made wooden casing. One of William's stone carvings hangs on the wall above the old pine chest.

ABOVE RIGHT It is no surprise to hear that William also made the showers, getting the glass cut specially to size. Wooden concertina drying racks hang on the wall outside this downstairs shower room and are invaluable for drying laundry when it is too wet to hang it outdoors.

OPPOSITE Downstairs, the rooms lead one into the other, with this playroom sandwiched between the kitchen and the living room. The sofa strikes an unusual note of almost urban sophistication in a house where so much is hand-made and where even the toys are appealingly vintage.

also made the two simple, sturdy oak staircases. Recently, a local landowner offered William and Sophie the trunk of a particularly venerable oak tree of immense girth. The broad planks are stacked while they season, waiting to be made into a floor for the most recent addition to the house. This is an adjoining barn, now converted to make a spacious office where Sophie can write (she is Associate Editor of *Resurgence* magazine), and compose her blog, which speaks eloquently of the pleasures of cooking, gardening, making and creating with her children Sacha aged 10, Robin aged 8 and Zoisa, who is 4.

Both she and William are passionate about the way of life they have forged here, so rich in hands-on experience, if a little Spartan and isolated for some tastes. 'I suppose you could call us 21st-century traditionalists,' Sophie muses. 'It's not that we want to go backwards – I couldn't work without a computer – but life for many children seems to have become so passive. It isn't always easy to live like this. When I wanted a table for my computer and William said he would make me one out of an old door that had washed up on the beach, I wished we could just go to IKEA and buy one. Sometimes doing things ourselves, and slowly, makes life really difficult, but if you have to wait for something, and live through the process of its creation, it is very satisfying. I think that is a feeling a lot of modern children never have a chance to enjoy.'

Lunch is salad with broad beans picked just before we eat from raised beds in the large greenhouse William built on the site of another old barn. There is home-made chutney and eggs from the chickens that peck in the courtyard, one with an accompanying eddy of fluffy chicks.

ABOVE and LEFT The fabric and wood sculptures on the wall in this spare bedroom were made by William when he ran a sculpture course in Corsica. The carved newel post of the staircase can just be seen through the door. The second staircase (left) leads up from the playroom.

Kittens sleep in a soft pile next to the Aga and Sophie's two donkeys, Amir and Hassan, can be lured with pieces of apple to thrust their heavy heads into the kitchen over the stable-style door.

The whole scene would be in danger of caricature if it were not for Sophie and William's readiness for self-parody, telling stories that undercut the rural idyll, such as the time they brushed the donkeys and let the chickens out to impress a prestigious client who arrived just in time to witness the bloody aftermath of a massacre by a marauding fox. William describes his decision to make the floor tiles for the kitchen as 'fringing on insanity', although he is pleased with the end result, and Sophie admits to finding life frustrating sometimes but says she has found a cure. 'I go outside and blast away on my trumpet, and the donkeys join in. Then I feel better,' she laughs.

THIS PAGE When William and Sophie bought the farmhouse, all the upstairs rooms seemed much smaller, as walls and ceilings had been boxed in. Taking down the ceilings to reveal the old roof timbers makes the rooms feel spacious and airy. As is also the case downstairs, rooms lead one into the other. From this spare bedroom above the living room at one end of the house, there is a view through the bathroom to the granite fireplace in the main bedroom beyond.

There have been Tamblyns at Botelet Farm in Cornwall since 1860 when Thomas Tamblyn took over the tenancy. His youngest son, Cyrus, was born at the farm in 1884, bought it in 1913 and lived there until he died in 1987. Cyrus's son David, born in 1924, and his wife Barbara still live at Botelet, as do their grown-up children Richard and Julie. For nearly 30 years until the death of Cyrus, three generations lived under the same roof. Now that Richard Tamblyn is getting married, this may soon be true once more.

ABOVE The approach to the farm is scattered with ancient granite gate posts and staddle-stones. Visitors enter the farmhouse at the back, through a porch and straight into the old kitchen. The front façade is to the left, overlooking the garden.

BELOW The brick kitchen fireplace has a long mantelshelf crowded with souvenirs from Richard's travels. The brick was made locally and is stamped with the place name Looe.

FAMILY BUSINESS

OPPOSITE ABOVE LEFT and THIS PAGE ABOVE LEFT
The idyllic view from one of the yurts extends down to the farmhouse across a field of grazing sheep.

OPPOSITE CENTRE LEFT A corrugated shed in the garden is Barbara Tamblyn's father's smoking shed, moved from its place in his garden where he used to hide in it to smoke cigarettes – the adult equivalent of smoking behind the bike shed.

OPPOSITE RIGHT The 'new' farmhouse was built after the landlord, Sir William Trelawny, fell through the floor of the old one, which still stands opposite, now beautifully restored and rented out as a holiday cottage.

The farm has gained another 70 acres since Thomas bought it, bringing its land up to 300 acres, much of it grazed by sheep and cattle, as it always was. The group of outbuildings, including a piggery, stables and barns, which date from the 17th to the 20th century, remain to one side of the farmhouse. Manor Cottage, which the new farmhouse was built to replace in 1884, faces its successor across a narrow yard. Even inside the farmhouse there is much that would be familiar to Thomas Tamblyn. The floors of the old kitchen, dairy and breakfast room retain their smooth slate flags, glossy as sealskin, and the brick fireplace is furnished with its original hooks and ratchets for cooking pots. The cloam (masonry) oven is still in working order and the table is the same that Cyrus and his father sat around with up to 13 family and farm labourers.

THIS PAGE and OPPOSITE
Richard converted the dairy at the back
of the house to make a new kitchen,
separate from the original kitchen
where bed and breakfast guests dine.
He incorporated as much of the low
slate shelving into the design as he
could and kept the wooden wall
shelving as storage. Pinned inside the
door of the blue china cupboard are
handwritten menus dating back to the
1940s when his grandparents used to
cater for visiting bus-loads of tourists.

Its top, which was always scrubbed every Monday, is still scrubbed, and underneath you can see maroon paint on the side that was turned uppermost for Sundays and special occasions. Upstairs there are bare boards in the bedrooms, a wooden four-poster in one and iron bedsteads in the other. The washbasins were installed in the 1920s, but water still comes from the spring deep under the orchard that has supplied the farm for centuries.

Little in this peaceful, unspoilt pocket of land seems to have changed in the last 150 years. What has changed is the way the Tamblyn family make a living from it. In the late 1980s, the family sold its herd of Charolais cattle, and instead rented out land to neighbouring farmers. First Manor Cottage, then Cowslip Cottage, both of which had been tenanted by farm labourers, became available and were renovated as holiday cottages.

More recently, the Tamblyns joined the Countryside Stewardship Scheme, work that keeps them busy all winter, planting trees, renewing hedges, restoring ancient walls and conserving the Neolithic hill fort that occupies the highest point of their land.

Far from being stuck in a time warp, 21st-century Botelet is a successful, stylish and modern enterprise with its very own beautifully designed website. Illustrated by Richard's evocative photographs, this advertises bed and organic breakfast in the farmhouse as well as self-catering accommodation in the cottages, camping in a wildflower meadow and even two yurts complete with cosy stoves, double beds and quirky vintage furniture. Also available are massage and reflexology, espresso coffee and Wi-Fi. Rustic it may be, but this combination of fresh air, wholesome food and farmhouse nostalgia is also in tune with the current appetite for unadorned, authentic, eco-friendly luxury.

Tamblyns have always been innovative and ready for a challenge. Cyrus Tamblyn was only the second person in the parish to own a car, and a photograph of him and his wife Ella sitting in it side by side, looking elegant and self-possessed, hangs in pride of place over the kitchen fireplace. Richard Tamblyn bred the first herd of Charolais cattle in Cornwall, and when he bought a combine harvester, he joined an elite group of five Cornish farmers who owned them.

ABOVE LEFT The brick fireplace in the original kitchen incorporates an old-fashioned cloam oven for baking. Richard was taught how to use it by a great aunt, who showed him how to heat it up by burning bundles of faggots inside it. Once heated through, the oven can be used for up to three hours. Richard helped his father to install the Rayburn range when he was 16, some 30 years ago.

ABOVE Two chairs made by a friend from old wooden pallets sit on either side of the fireplace.

OPPOSITE The floor is slate, which was traditionally sealed with milk, poured on and quickly wiped off. The table top has been trimmed, but it was once big enough to seat 13 family and farm labourers.

ABOVE LEFT In the room that was Julie Tamblyn's childhood bedroom, Richard has picked out a rough map of Cornwall in the layers of old paint above the metal bed, and stuck a wooden frame to the wall around it.

LEFT, ABOVE and OPPOSITE In the main bedroom, Richard has left a paint shadow like the ghost of the old chimneypiece, which his parents removed when they 'modernized' the house in the 1950s. The bed was bought from a reclamation yard where they claimed it had once belonged to Nelson's mistress, Lady Hamilton. The ladder seen through the door leads to the attic bedroom (left) where Richard and his fiancée Tia retreat to make space for summer guests.

He is probably the first Cornish farmer in his eighties to have taken up writing a blog. And Richard has just installed two wind turbines to generate green energy.

Tamblyns are also hoarders, and remarkably creative when it comes to recycling. In the 1960s, David and Barbara bought a railway banana-wagon and converted it to make a compact holiday home, which they rented out complete with fold-down bed and television. As children, Richard and Julie visited it to watch *Thunderbirds*, for which they couldn't get reception in the farmhouse. Everywhere you look there are things made from other things, whether the garden summerhouse constructed by Richard entirely using bits and pieces found on the farm down to the last nail; the garden table made from the slate base of a water tank on granite roller legs; or the eccentric lighting in the house, its wiring contained in snaking segments of old lead pipe.

Richard is largely responsible for the look of the place. Like Julie, he considers himself fortunate to have been brought up on

a farm where mending and making things was second nature. He is a self-taught craftsman-builder with a natural eye for order and beauty, and his conversion of the dairy with its limewashed walls and low slate shelving to make a new kitchen is an object lesson in sensitive restoration. He works slowly, often leaving something unfinished for so long that he decides he likes it as it is, such as the stripped plaster, which still bears the imprint of the old patterned wallpaper in the breakfast room that is now his office, or the painted shadow of the chimneypiece that was removed by his parents when they modernized the main bedroom in the 1950s. Above the bed in the second bedroom is what appears to be a framed map. In fact, it is an image scraped from the layers of old paint, including a yellow hue dating from when this was Julie's childhood bedroom. 'When I started stripping the walls, I came to a patch that reminded me of the shape of Cornwall,' Richard explains, 'so I helped it along a bit and found some wood to make a frame for it.'

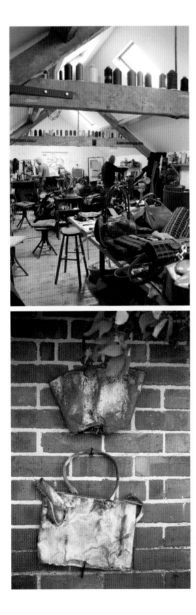

HOUSE OF LEATHER

Hanging on a peg in Matt and Jax Fothergill's kitchen is a python-skin bag so large and luxurious that you would automatically assume it to be fake. In fact, it is the genuine article and was a present to Jax from Matt, who made it from a snakeskin that stretched the entire length of his workshop. The workshop is a long room, lit by large skylights and converted from a hayloft above stables and a cart shed, in a barn situated behind the house. The snake must have measured a good 30 feet.

Matt Fothergill has been working with tanned animal skin in its many forms since he graduated from London's Cordwainers College, where he studied saddlery and harness making. After serving an apprenticeship with shoemakers Edward Green, and a stint doing repairs at historic department store Liberty, where he met Jax who was 'selling posh socks', he set up on his own, supplying upmarket shops that include The Conran Shop, Paul Smith and Nicole Farhi. Currently, he is working on a batch of black leather kit bags for a firm of City of London lawyers, and a range of souvenir goods for London Transport, using leather together with their iconic moquette fabrics to create bags, bolster cushions and travelcard holders.

Climbing up the steep, wooden staircase to the big, light space where Matt works with his colleague Andy Kirkbride, you pass a kangaroo skin hung over the stairwell, and more snakeskins pinned to the wall, the natural geometry of their scales glinting like semi-precious stones. There are hides of every description, but also big bolts of fabric instantly recognizable from the seats of London buses and tube trains, and a little incongruous in this context so far removed from the commuter crush, here on the edge of a small Shropshire town.

ABOVE A home-made game pie makes a delicious lunch with tomatoes from the greenhouse, and salad from the vegetable garden.

LEFT Matt's colleague Andy took on the unenviable task of stripping generations of gloss paint off the original cast-iron fireplace in the living room, a room that has also retained its original flagged floor. Many of the furnishings are leather, including the sofa, the cushions, the beanbag and the curtain tie-backs.

OPPOSITE When Jax and Matt bought the house this room was being used as a living room, but the large fireplace, bread oven and larder cupboard tucked next to the chimney breast and now dismantled show that it was designed to be the kitchen. Leading off the kitchen is the back porch, invariably used as the entrance to the house instead of the front door. The sweet peas are from the garden and the kitchen chairs are upholstered in glamorous sky blue leather.

Converting the workshop was a priority when Matt and Jax first bought the property ten years ago. The move from their house on the Isle of Dogs in London's East End to a part of the country that the poet A.E. Housman described as one of the 'quietest places under the sun' was a decisive shift from full-on urban to the unequivocally rural. But their daughter Holly, aged eight, was desperate to own a pony, Matt describes himself as 'very keen on hunting, shooting and fishing' and Jax wanted a garden where she could grow vegetables and keep chickens. One day, while visiting Matt's parents on the edge of Ludlow, they drove past the house and saw the 'For Sale' sign. They viewed the house the next day and realized they could relocate Matt's workshop to the barn, and make a family home with all the space they needed, plus pony.

Matt stayed in London to work, while Jax and Holly moved into a house that had hardly changed since it was built in the 1880s.

THIS PAGE Upstairs there are two main bedrooms at the front on either side of the staircase, both still with their servant's bell pulls, one of which attaches to a bell in Holly's room at the back where the maid once slept. Matt and Jax's bedroom is dominated by an Edwardian bedstead in Arts and Crafts style. All the woodwork, including floorboards, has been painstakingly stripped of old paint and varnish.

LEFT Looking across the foot of Matt and Jax's bed to the tiny original fireplace, which can only have held a handful of coals and produced very minimal warmth on a cold winter's night. The partial matchboarding is also original. The canvas and leather holdall on the floor is one of Matt's designs.

RIGHT In the bathroom they have used reclaimed slate tiles from when they repaired the roof to surround the bathtub and washbasin, and to line a shower. In this room Matt has used blue suede as a window curtain.

'It belonged to a local farmer who owned several farms, and came here to retire and run a smallholding,' says Jax. 'The man who had last lived here with his daughter died aged 104 and the house had a really old-fashioned feel. The exterior was covered in pebble-dash with everything else painted bright turquoise. Inside it was almost Victorian, with the servants' bells still in working order, patterned wallpapers and all the woodwork covered in sticky, brown varnish or painted dark green and mustard. There was no central heating and I had to get up at five in the morning to light the Rayburn [range] if I wanted to be able to cook an egg for breakfast.'

Once the hayloft was ready, Matt and Andy made the move from London, and work began on the house. After plumbing, rewiring, reroofing, moving the kitchen and rearranging the bathroom, the daunting task of decorating could finally begin. 'Stripping paint became our evening leisure activity,' Jax jokes. 'And the walls were covered with layer upon layer of wallpaper. I kept samples of them and they're like a history of fashion in interior design, from sludgy browns right through to the psychedelic flowers of the '70s.'

Most of the walls needed replastering, but the wall in the kitchen opposite the Aga was sound and they decided to leave it in its freshly stripped state, mottled and marbled with colours and papers from the last 130 years. Elsewhere, walls are painted in pale, neutral shades and the old doors, cupboards and floorboards have been taken back to the bare wood. Furnishings are simple, with an Arts and Crafts feel, and an impressive collection of *objets trouvés*, dating back to their mudlarking days on the banks of the Thames and including stoneware bottles and clay pipes, clusters on mantelpieces and windowsills.

Perfectly in tune with the theme of natural materials and neutral colours is the use of leather, not just to upholster chairs, sofas, stools and beanbags but also as curtains in the hall and bathroom, covering cushions and the coffee table, and woven to make tie-backs at the living room window. There are also leather doorstops, a leather draught excluder, a leather fly swat, leather washbags and leather coats and jackets hanging in the porch, all of them made by Matt and Andy. There is even an apron of brown snakeskin hanging in front of the butler's sink in the utility room. And that's before you start on the handbags.

ORGANIC FARMHOUSE
elements of style

- **MAKE YOUR OWN** Sculptor William Peers and his father Robin have successfully made all manner of things for William and Sophie's farmhouse, from staircases to floor tiles. The floor tiles were a particularly impressive feat of DIY, from the digging of the local clay and the making of the wooden moulds to the construction of the kiln. William has also used Cornish slate for splashbacks behind sinks and for window sills. While making your own floor tiles might be a step too far, the principle of using locally sourced materials, whether wood, stone or clay, gives a house a connection with its surroundings that is one of the appealing characteristics of vernacular architecture.

- **STRIPPING BACK** Stripping old plaster and leaving the resulting surface with its mottled layers of paint and fragments of paper as in Matt and Jax Fothergill's kitchen is so fashionable that a version of it now features in Jamie Oliver's restaurant in Bath. At its best it is a very attractive finish, with all the variegations and modulations of colour of a slice of marble. Richard Tamblyn has taken it further by picking away at layers of old paint in a bedroom to create a shape resembling a map of Cornwall, around which he has glued wooden mouldings as a frame. Framing a particularly interesting segment of a stripped wall is a way to preserve a small piece of decorating history if you don't want to leave the whole wall naked.

- **FINDERS KEEPERS** Matt and Jax Fothergill used to live next to the River Thames and often went mudlarking at low tide. Their house is decorated with many of their finds, including broken clay pipes dating back to the 17th century and stoneware bottles. Outside, they have made equally attractive displays of found sheep and deer skulls and rusting horseshoes, while old zinc buckets and watering cans, too far gone for use, have been hammered flat to hang on the walls of the barn as rustic decoration.

- **TAKING TIME** All the houses in this chapter have taken years rather than weeks or months to renovate and decorate. Richard Tamblyn took four years to convert the old farm dairy into a kitchen and is a great believer in living with each stage of change before moving on. 'Sometimes, I decide I like something just as it is,' he comments, citing the mark left on the wall where the mantelpiece was removed in his parents' old bedroom. Instead of painting over the mark, he has left its ghostly outline. 'If you always rush at things,' he says, 'you can miss something beautiful.'

- **HUMBLE MATERIALS** Sometimes, a humble material works just as well as an extravagant one. The campsite shower room in an outbuilding at Botelet is lined with corrugated iron, while cardboard boxes lined up on the kitchen floor are used to separate household waste for recycling. Both are practical and good-looking.

I see the barns and comely manors planned
By men who somehow moved in comely thought,
Who, with a simple shippon to their hand,
As men upon some godlike business wrought

JOHN DRINKWATER (1882–1937)

TRADITIONAL
FARMHOUSE

A TRADITIONAL FARMHOUSE HAS A KITCHEN DRESSER, A FLAGSTONE FLOOR AND AN AGA FOR THE SUNDAY ROAST. A TRADITIONAL FARM HAS CHICKENS PECKING AND BOBBING IN AND OUT OF THE BARNS, PIGS IN THE YARD, COWS IN THE MILKING PARLOUR, SHEEP IN THE FIELDS AND CLOTTED CREAM IN THE FRIDGE. NONE OF THE HOUSES IN THIS CHAPTER HAVE ALL THESE THINGS; NONE OF THEM ARE WORKING FARMS. BUT THEY EACH HAVE ELEMENTS OF THE OLD-FASHIONED ROMANCE THAT MADE US FALL IN LOVE WITH FARMYARDS WHEN WE WERE CHILDREN AND WHICH MAKES US DREAM OF LIVING IN THE COUNTRY WHEN WE ARE GROWN-UP.

THIS PAGE A map dating from 1629 shows that the front of the farmhouse was originally on the other side, where it was approached by a track from the river. The oldest part of the house is the wing on the right, which incorporates a window dating from 1400 found under layers of lath and plaster when the house was restored and rescued from near dereliction in 1969.

OPPOSITE ABOVE LEFT and RIGHT The herringbone brick on a back wall dates from the early 16th century, when the two-storey cross-wing, or solar, which can be seen opposite above right, was added.

OPPOSITE BELOW RIGHT Grass steps lead up the sloping lawn.

OPPOSITE BOTTOM RIGHT The steep gable of the east wing incorporates pigeon-holes.

A WARM WELCOME

A map of Finstock Farm in Sussex dated 1629 has at its centre a drawing of a double-gabled farmhouse next to a cluster of tiny outbuildings, like a mother with her babies. To the south of the house are fields colour-coded to show different crops, and to the north are groups of diminutive animals, neatly labelled, including horses, sheep, deer and rabbit warrens, or 'Cunny Buris'. Another label, with accompanying illustration, says 'Turfe here cutte' and nearby 'Fearne here cutte'. Surrounding this patch of cultivated land is common land. The map is a graphic glimpse of farm life in the early 17th century and a reminder of how much common land was once available for grazing, fuel and general foraging for those without land of their own.

Arriving at Finstock today, up the bumpy track that leads past its barns, the house exudes old English charm with its slightly crooked half-timbering, mullioned windows and leaded lights, its steep, clay-tiled roof and towering, brick chimneys. The barns, which date from the 18th century and replaced the haphazard scatter of outbuildings shown on the map, have been converted to make a separate property, and a small barn huddled next to the house has become a cottage. Behind the house the piggery and another barn are falling into disrepair. But there are chickens in the garden and horses stabled just over the fence, and it doesn't take much imagination to picture this as the home of a wealthy yeoman farmer feasting on rabbit pie, venison steaks and the plump birds that nested in the pigeon-holes piercing one of the gables.

Maggie Hadfield and her late husband Michael first spotted Finstock Farm over 40 years ago. 'We lived in a village not far from here,' she reminisces, 'and walking through the woods we used to see this romantic, derelict house that had obviously been uninhabited for some time. When the estate decided to sell the house, we longed to buy it, but you couldn't get a mortgage in those days for something in such disrepair. However, I knew the lady who did buy it, and our children were friends. She spent two years restoring it and one day when we visited, and my children were rushing around the garden and saying how much they wished we lived here, she turned to me and said that if we would like to buy it she would sell the house to us without putting it on the market. She said she found it too lonely.'

It was an irresistible offer, so in the early 1970s, Maggie, Michael and their four young children upped sticks and moved into the house they all loved. Michael worked locally as a solicitor, but Maggie stayed at home with the children and animals, including at one stage a small flock of sheep. A photograph of a favourite ewe called Cloud, who has a particularly kindly face and featured on their Christmas card, stands propped on the kitchen dresser.

ABOVE LEFT The accoutrements of country pursuits are stored under the stairs just inside the front door. Maggie's granddaughter Lily, who lives with her mother in the converted barn next to the house, is a keen rider.

ABOVE The timber wall at the end of the kitchen is medieval, the room beyond it a much later addition.

OPPOSITE At the other end of the kitchen, the four-oven Aga is dwarfed by the Tudor brick fireplace it tucks into. The table is made from planks of elm, cut from trees that died from Dutch elm disease, jointed by a local carpenter. The beech kitchen cupboards date back to when the house was restored in the late 1960s.

Next to it is a photograph of Henny, the big ginger hen who used to come into the kitchen when she heard the theme tune to *Friends*, perch on the back of a kitchen chair to watch it and promptly fall fast asleep. Then there was Henry, the castrated ram, who Maggie says was a brilliant ball-player and could head a football kicked in his direction, and also enjoyed sledging down the slope of the garden lawn when it snowed.

The sheep have gone now, but the interior of the farmhouse is not very different from when they first bought it; simply restored, plumbed, wired and with handsome beech joinery installed in the kitchen. This large, light room is in the oldest part of the house, and was originally a two-storey, timber-framed hall. Parts of this room date back as far as 1400, including a small medieval window with wooden mullions that, Maggie says, would originally have been covered by a flap of leather rather than shutters. Some time at the beginning of the 17th century,

OPPOSITE BELOW The dining room and music room is in the part of the house that dates from the 16th century. The fireplace alcove, which would have shared a flue with the kitchen fireplace, has been furnished with an 18th-century oak sideboard with a Regency gilt mirror resting on it. The door seen across the hall to the right opens into the kitchen.

OPPOSITE ABOVE In a corner of the drawing room, an early 18th-century wall cupboard is home to a 17th-century shoe that was discovered hidden in the chimney when the house was restored. It would have originally been placed there by the builders as a charm to ward off evil spirits.

ABOVE In the summertime, a pretty Victorian tray hides the blank face of the wood-burning stove in the living room. This room is in the early 17th-century stone-built wing of the house, and dates from the time the map entitled 'John Mille his house and lande' was drawn.

a stone-built wing was added containing the winding wooden staircase, and at the same time the wide brick kitchen fireplace and broad chimney stack were inserted, all of which remain intact.

Unlike so many old houses whose external architecture is undercut by over-restored interiors stripped of any character, the beams, bricks, floors and woodwork are beautifully weathered and worn with age and use, a patina carefully preserved by the architects who rescued the house from dereliction.

THIS PICTURE The winding oak staircase was installed at the beginning of the 17th century and incorporates small wall cupboards in its central core. This is the first floor landing and the stairs continue up another flight to further rooms in the attic. Old leather hat boxes and suitcases sit on the wide oak stair treads.

ABOVE In one of the first floor bedrooms that Maggie lets out to bed and breakfast guests, the timber wall beams frame a bedhead made from fabric pinned to a cross beam with a heading of fabric rosettes. Charming Regency watercolours of flowers are sprinkled across the walls.

LEFT The attic is piled with vintage and antique clothes collected by Maggie, ideal for games of dressing up when her grandchildren visit.

OPPOSITE ABOVE A bedroom at the front of the house is presided over by a stately half-tester bed made from sections of old panelling.

OPPOSITE BELOW In the same bedroom, books and old albums are piled on a chest at the end of the bed, and a sofa provides an inviting place to curl up and read them.

Furnished with an unpretentious mix of inherited antiques and pictures, Finstock has the comfortable, settled feel of a house that has been lived in and enjoyed for many years. Maggie's musical talent is represented by the grand piano, soon to be replaced by a more compact English square piano that she has just had restored. 'I would love to have been a professional singer,' she confesses, 'but my father was a parson, so I had to earn a living.' Instead, she sings locally in a choir, chamber groups and as a soloist.

Fifteen years ago when her husband died, Maggie decided to start offering bed and breakfast, 'partly as a way to justify staying here, but also because it is nice to share the house with other people'. One of her sons lives in a nearby village, and Kate Blunt, her daughter, who inherited artistic genes from her father's side of the family and works as a portrait painter (her work can be seen on page 192), lives in the cottage converted from a barn right next to the house and has a studio in a shed at the top of the garden. They have two dogs, Bella, a wire-haired terrier, and Lola, a Jack Russell puppy, and Kate's daughter Lily is a keen rider. So there are still children and animals at Finstock, and still fresh eggs for breakfast.

THIS PAGE The picturesque façade of the farmhouse dates from the late 16th century, but it was originally built elsewhere as the wing of a much larger house. A formal rose garden at the front is enclosed by clipped box. Separated from the house by an expanse of lawn is an orchard. When the estate was purchased by William Gibson's grandfather in 1894, the house was recorded as having an orchard of 150 fruit trees, only four of which have survived to this day. To the right of the house are extensive farm buildings including a huge barn that once housed a sizeable dairy herd with an unusual strutwork roof (see OPPOSITE). Today the house is used as a weekend and holiday retreat, and this barn provides garaging and storage.

Flying in the face of the old adage, some fortunate people contrive to enjoy the best of both worlds. Lori and William Gibson own a grand, central London house where they live during the week, but almost every weekend, and for longer in the summer months, they drive 30 miles, leaving behind the city's congestion and pavements, to their farmhouse in a remote and peaceful corner of a large estate that has been owned by various branches of William's family for just over 100 years.

MODEL MAKEOVER

The house looks as though it has sat here in its setting of fields and copses since it was built in the late 16th century, its façade of plain stone with mullioned windows enlivened at its centre by a sudden burst of architectural ebullience in the shape of two pointed gables, one above the other, the lower a porch, the upper a projecting bay that rises into the roof where it becomes a dormer window. Both gables are decorated with a trio of tall finials, each topped by a stone ball. Red and white roses froth around the windows and precisely clipped box hedging encloses a

formal front garden, beyond which spreads an expanse of lawn that has been mowed into broad stripes like a giant green-on-green wallpaper.

In fact, the building was originally sited some distance away and started life as the wing of a much larger house, Wakehurst Place. It was moved here by its wealthy Victorian owner, stone by stone, beam by beam, in the mid-19th century to make a picturesque home for a tenant farmer. Wakehurst Place is none the worse for the amputation, while its former wing has settled very comfortably into its new landscape.

Further proof that money was no object is the range of late-Victorian outbuildings grouped to one side of the farmhouse. While the house embodies old-fashioned charm, the outbuildings must have been state-of-the-art when they were built to accommodate a substantial dairy herd, and to store and process industrial quantities of feed. The largest of the buildings has an elaborate wooden strutwork roof and the whole complex is beautifully designed to maximize efficiency. The main barn was used as a milking parlour until about 20 years ago when Lori and William took possession of the house, at which point the working farm was relocated.

The farmhouse had been divided up into two parts, with one side inhabited by the farmer and his wife, and the other by the wife's parents, and Lori describes the original interior as 'a complete rabbit warren of small, interconnecting rooms'. Lori is American, grew up in Miami, worked in advertising in Washington D.C. for 13 years, and moved to London 24 years ago when she met and married William. She is also an anglophile with a passionate appreciation of architectural history and period style.

THIS PAGE The drawing room walls are painted a fresh apple green with curtains in a rosy chintz by Colefax and Fowler. Furnishings are a comfortable mix of antiques and traditional upholstery. These rooms were decorated nearly 20 years ago, but the style is classic English country house, and sidesteps the pitfalls of fashion. As the Gibsons' decorator Guy Oliver of Oliver Laws says, the interior of the house has a 'timeless quality'.

Lori's vision for the interior of the farmhouse was 'to create a traditional look appropriate to the informality of the house, without pomp or grandeur'.

With the help of interior designers Oliver Laws – a firm that can count the state rooms at 10 Downing Street among its many prestigious commissions – she has succeeded. Rooms were opened out with the judicious removal of internal walls to give a rational layout of dining room and drawing room on either side of the staircase, and a kitchen and conservatory at the back of the house that open onto the garden, which has been beautifully landscaped to include a shaded terrace for alfresco dining and a sheltered swimming pool. Inside, the decoration is classic English country house without the merest, modish nod to contemporary fashion; pretty, unpretentious and comfortable. There are framed oil paintings on the walls, gently faded rugs on the floors and plumply upholstered chairs and sofas at every turn. Lifting the style from predictable to delightful are the colour schemes – fresh apple green walls in the drawing room and Colefax curtains scattered with big, pink roses; a yellow bedroom dressed with mossy green tartan; and a main bedroom in softest shades of blue and bursts of mustard yellow.

So far, so very English. But, just as the Gibsons seem to enjoy the best of town and country, so they have managed to combine some of the finest attributes of interior design and domestic luxury from both their native countries. Not only are the bathrooms in the house beautifully furnished, in the mould of Nancy Lancaster's 'little works of art', but if you cross the courtyard to the outbuildings nearest the house, you will find they have been converted to make a dining room and kitchen for large-scale entertaining, a modern gym and a huge, panelled games room with a billiard table, as well as a fully equipped cinema with specially made plush seating.

The transformation from working farm to country retreat has been effected with a mix of American panache and English restraint. Lori and William's children Matthew and Sarah are now at university, but the family continues to gather here; William loves walking, Lori gardens and there is no shortage of entertainment for the children and their friends.

OPPOSITE and ABOVE The original late 16th-century house, which began life as a wing of Wakehurst Place, was only one room deep, which explains why this spare bedroom at the back of the house features a stone mullioned window in a wall that was once an outer wall. When the house was dismantled and then rebuilt on its present site, it was doubled in size thanks to the addition of a range of rooms all along the back. The bedroom is decorated with strips of a rosy wallpaper border by Mauny, and here, as elsewhere in the house, a punchy mustard yellow adds bite to an otherwise gentle colour scheme of muted shades of blue, mauve and purple. The same potent yellow tone is picked up in the dainty pleated lampshade and the background of a chintz cushion on the blue armchair.

THIS PAGE A spare bedroom is decorated in a more masculine style with yellow walls, tartan curtains, a Victorian brass bed and oak furniture. The view across the landing looks through the main bedroom and into its bathroom beyond. This bedroom mirrors the arrangement and also has its own bathroom.

RESTORATION DRAMA

In 2008, antiques dealers Doris Urquhart and Christopher Richardson took possession of the largest and most expensive antique they had ever bought. What appealed about it was its great age, and the fact that, although many additions had been made to it over the years, they could see that most of its original fabric remained intact. What they had not bargained for was quite how long it would take to remove its later accretions, or how difficult a job it would be. It was, after all, a house, not a piece of furniture – a long, timber-framed Suffolk farmhouse – so it was going to take more than spit, polish and a toolbox to put right.

OPPOSITE The house is one room deep and the front door opens into a large space that Doris and Christopher use as a kitchen and dining room. They think it was once a workshop, which goes some way to explaining the patchwork flooring, incorporating bricks, terracotta floor tiles, the occasional stone slab and planks of wood.

THIS PAGE The front of the house presents a flat façade with three front doors that date back to the time when it was divided to make cottages and a workshop. At the rear, shown here, there are two extensions – a two-storey Regency extension that contains a bathroom on the first floor and a small sitting room beneath, and a single-storey extension that was used as a dairy and is probably the oldest part of the house. The black clapboard barn next to the house is a shop at the front and a delightful holiday cottage at the back.

Stories of other people's painful and painstaking house restorations can sometimes be as tedious as wading through the unedited longueurs of their holiday snaps. But even if you are not particularly fascinated by ancient, vernacular architecture, the humour, enthusiasm and knowledge with which Doris and Christopher tell their tale – whether of a ceiling, a chimney and a single-storey extension collapsing, or taking baths in a room with holes in it protected from the elements by nothing more than some plastic sheeting – are enough to keep you on the very edge of your seat. That and the intriguing, patchwork beauty of the house itself.

As with most very old houses, the architectural history is complicated. The earliest part of the house is a room that leads off the living room, which has a medieval window, now blocked up, with wooden mullions.

This single-storey space was once a separate dwelling, 'a tiny little hovel', as Doris puts it in her forthright, American way. Later, the hovel aggrandized into a hall house with the addition of a large, two-storey space and a hearth in the middle. In the 16th century, the hall was divided to make an upstairs and a downstairs, and at some point the medieval hovel was converted to make a dairy, with a drain in its brick floor for the water used to cool the milk, butter and cheese. Later still, the house was divided into two separate cottages and a workshop, hence the oddity of the three front doors along the façade.

Clues to how the house has been used over the centuries are imprinted in its fabric. It was certainly a farm. Doris and Christopher have rebuilt the barn that sits at right angles to the house and which had fallen into ruin. With its black weatherboarding, reclaimed pantiles, windows and door, the new building looks almost as old as the freshly painted house

ABOVE The inglenook in the drawing room had been blocked in with some of the bricks that have now been reused as flooring. Walls, ceilings and beams are painted in a uniform coat of Farrow & Ball distemper in Cord. The bench in front of the fireplace is 16th century.

LEFT Next to the kitchen and dining room is the drawing room, with a floor of reclaimed bricks laid in the traditional manner on sand by Doris and Christopher. Doris says you don't need to clean the floor because the dirt just disappears down the gaps. The primitive Tudor portrait of a three-year-old boy hanging to the right of the door is one of Doris's favourite possessions.

RIGHT The battered workbench beneath the long kitchen window makes a sturdy work surface.

beside it, and is big enough to accommodate a spacious antiques shop at one end and a charming, two-bedroom holiday cottage at the other. The dairy is the other most obvious legacy of life on the farm, and the garden is still ringed by cows grazing peacefully on the surrounding marshland.

At the end of the house where they have made their kitchen there is a hefty, battered workbench. Up a narrow wooden staircase next to the dining table is a room Doris uses as a study.

Please do not
Gather the flowers

THIS PICTURE At the
working end of the kitchen,
Doris and Christopher have
installed an Aga on the wall
opposite the original
workbench, but anachronistic
appliances are hidden in a
room of their own through the
planked door to the right of the
dresser. The uncomfortable tilt
of the painted cupboard is due
to the uneven gradient of the
floor. The wooden staircase
leads up to Doris's study.

ABOVE Doris cannot resist old toys, especially dolls and stuffed animals, which line the mantelpiece in the main bedroom and slump on chairs. The floors upstairs slope so violently that the bed has to be propped on fat chunks of wood to ensure its occupants do not roll out of it in their sleep.

LEFT A set of small wall shelves in the dairy display Georgian glasses, which are regularly used by Doris and Christopher.

OPPOSITE The oldest part of the house is this single-storey room with a medieval wooden mullioned window, now blocked in. This is the original 'hovel', which was later used as a dairy when the house was a farm. It was this room, with its ancient, gimcrack shelving and slatted, wooden partitioning, that first convinced Doris and Christopher to buy the house.

Here, beams and walls are coated with a knobbly porridge of dried paint, wiped and splashed over the course of many years. 'We think it may have been a carter's or a wheelwright's workshop,' says Doris, 'and perhaps this is why the brick floor is so broken, and parts of it have been replaced with blocks and planks of wood where the hooves of waiting horses have damaged it.' The ceiling beams at this end of the house are punctured with fat nails and crude hooks, and you can imagine them once festooned with the tools of whatever trade was plied here.

When Doris and Christopher first bought the farmhouse, much of its history was hidden. Soft pulpboard had been used to line and straighten up walls and ceilings, and clumsy concrete-block partitions had been inserted to create extra rooms. As they stripped away the layers, including acres of carpet and underlay, there was both good news and bad.

ABOVE Upstairs, the floorboards have been mended with strips of tin tacked over the gaps between them. A door on the left leads up to the small attic room where Doris imagines the maid once slept. Doris collects Victorian doll's houses, which she uses as wall cupboards. The doorway on the right opens into a bathroom.

TOP RIGHT This wooden staircase leads from the kitchen up to Doris's study, where the walls are encrusted with dried paint dating back to when this part of the house was a workshop.

ABOVE RIGHT Three French milliner's heads, originally used for displaying bonnets, on top of a cupboard containing creamware.

OPPOSITE This is the bathroom where Doris and Christopher took baths while the wind whistled through holes in the walls. The creamware plates on the wall are barber's basins with semi-circle cut-outs so that they can be held against a person's neck while being shaved by a barber. The floor is painted in Terre d'Egypte from Farrow & Ball.

More and more of the old house was revealed, but so was a long list of problems, from sopping wet beams and broken guttering to a towering pile of twigs and bird lime accumulated by generations of jackdaws nesting in the roof that was threatening to plummet right through the ceiling.

'We moved in and lived in one room,' Christopher recalls, 'and our standards of what was habitable dropped to nothing. The living room floor was a sandpit, and we had to pick our way over piles of rubble to get from one room to another, ducking under scaffolding that was holding the ceilings up. It was permanently dusty and we developed all kinds of itches and minor skin irritations.' Fortunately, there were also highs, like finding all the original floorboards upstairs, complete with the old strips of tin used to mend them, and taking out the brick infill to reveal the soot-encrusted interior of the Tudor inglenook.

Now finished and furnished, the house is serene, its lumps and bumps unified under a coating of Farrow & Ball distemper, its brick floors restored, gently wavering from kitchen, through dining room and into living room, while upstairs its floorboards, free of carpeting, rock and sway to a slightly different rhythm.

Doris and Christopher's furniture ideally complements the homely, picturesque architecture of these time-worn spaces; simple, country pieces, most dating from the 18th century or earlier. Christopher has an eye for elegance, but Doris is always attracted to the personal, whether it be a Regency child's desk with the name Anna Christmas written on the side, a primitive Tudor portrait of a chubby-cheeked three-year-old or a stuffed elephant with a slightly hangdog demeanour. Like the house itself, Doris describes them as 'things made for ordinary people, that make us feel connected with them and the lives they lived'.

RIGHT When Doris and Christopher bought the house, the barn was in ruins. They have rebuilt it, using reclaimed windows, doors and roof tiles, and use the front half as their shop. Here, they sell the country antiques they both love, including the doll's houses that Doris likes to use as cupboards, and Regency and early Victorian portrait silhouettes, of which they have their own extensive collection in the house. Walls and ceiling are painted in Farrow & Ball's Terre d'Egypte.

'I am embarrassed to admit that we stalked this house for about two years before we bought it,' says Andrew Blackman, sitting at the desk in his study next to a view of lawn sloping away to fields and a fringe of trees, behind which a broad stripe of sea shimmers like polished pewter. The sea is the English Channel, and the house is a grand old farmhouse sitting high above the town of Hastings at the top of a steep and beautiful valley that points its tilting arrow down to a tiny beach of rocks and shingle.

CLIFF-TOP RESCUE

This is the same view that Andrew and his partner Richard Smith enjoyed as they sat in front of the house eating their picnic having first found it, boarded up and semi-derelict, on an exploratory detour from a coastal walk. 'We had a weekend house in Tonbridge, not far from here, and lived and worked in London,' Andrew explains. 'But we often came walking across the cliffs and when we spotted this we thought it was perfect. After that we used to visit it quite regularly.' The house had been empty for several years and comprehensively vandalized. However, local enquiries revealed it was likely to come on the market before too long.

When eventually they heard that the house was to be sold at auction, Andrew and Richard were away on holiday. An added complication was that the date of the auction coincided with their annual Christmas drinks party, for which invitations had already been sent out. Andrew took responsibility for attending the auction and bidding – an activity for which he has had years of practice as a dealer specializing in old master paintings – and Richard stayed at home to organize the party. With admirable good sense, they fixed on a price and agreed not to exceed it.

ABOVE The front half of the house dates from the 17th century, although the central porch and new front door were added in the mid-19th century. The window above the porch is Richard and Andrew's bathroom, and affords a magnificent view of the sea.

OPPOSITE and BELOW RIGHT The entrance hall opens into the double drawing room to the right and Andrew's study to the left. The original inglenook fireplace in the drawing room dates from when the house was first built. The wallpaper in the hall is Garthwaite, a design by Richard for his own company Madeaux (available through Tissus d'Helene) and is in a custom colour with a metallic silver background to reflect light. A door at the back of the hall opens into the windowless central corridor that separates the older house at the front from the Georgian additions.

OPPOSITE ABOVE LEFT The dining room is presided over by a huge map of Sussex dating from 1824.

OPPOSITE CENTRE LEFT A mantelpiece in a spare bedroom enlivened by butterflies and flowers.

OPPOSITE BELOW LEFT The sandstone from which the house is built varies from soft yellow to pink.

ABOVE All the fabrics in the house are designs by Richard Smith. In the drawing room the curtains are Large Peonies from Warner Fabrics at Zimmer & Rohde, trimmed with green velvet ribbon borders and lined with a fine ticking stripe.

RIGHT Facing the inglenook in the drawing room is a tall folding screen covered in Bazaar from Madeaux. Paintwork in French Gray from Farrow & Ball creates a neutral background for the rich colours and textures of cushions and upholstery.

Despite huge interest in the house and an inexplicably high attendance at the auction, the bidding stopped just short of their limit. 'It was the best Christmas drinks party we ever had,' Andrew grins. 'We were just so pleased and surprised to have bought it.'

A beauty parade of more than a dozen builders, architects and historic buildings specialists was won hands down by a local builder whom they unanimously describe as 'lovely': 'He was enthusiastic and positive, and we knew he was the right person.' His first task was to put on a new roof. One of the leaks was so

severe that Richard says it was like having an indoor water feature when it rained, with a mini waterfall cascading down one of the drawing room walls. Once the roof was finished, they set to work to make the kitchen at the back of the house habitable and installed an Aga to begin the process of drying out the sodden plaster and floors.

As the work progressed, Richard and Andrew moved out of the caravan they used for weekend visits and into rooms in the attic, and from there into the newly renovated annexe, which is now separate accommodation and home to one of the builders who worked on it. Finally, they abandoned London altogether. With space for Richard, who works as a freelance textile designer, to have a studio and an office, and for Andrew to have a study from which to run his business, they decided to make this their permanent and only home.

As in all the best partnerships, they share out the tasks. When it comes to decorating, 'Andrew is furniture and paintings,' says Richard, 'and I am fabrics and colours.' Pictures include a huge and detailed map, dating from 1824, of Sussex and its coastline, featuring Brighton labelled with its old name of Brighthelmstone. There are also 19th-century oils and watercolours of local views and landscapes. One particularly fascinating watercolour in the drawing room shows a celebration for Queen Victoria's accession to the throne in 1837 hosted by a previous owner of the house, showing hundreds of bonneted and frock-coated guests, sitting in a field at rows of long benches. The farmer who lived here and farmed the 800 acres the house once presided over must have been an extremely generous host.

The colours that Richard has chosen to provide a background to the pictures and furnishings are a subtle spectrum of Farrow & Ball neutrals and soft, knocked-back shades, whether gentle French Gray in the double drawing room, sophisticated Light Blue in the entrance hall or tawny Dauphin in a guest bathroom. Chosen with the eye of an expert colourist, the plain walls and woodwork perfectly frame and complement the fabrics of the curtains, bed hangings and upholstery, all of which are Richard's own textile designs.

OPPOSITE The kitchen at the back of the house overlooks a cobbled courtyard where farm labourers would come to collect their wages. The walls are painted in Fawn and the kitchen dresser with glass sliding doors in Dauphin, both by Farrow & Ball. The herringbone brick floor tiles are hand-made Polish roofing tiles, and were particularly difficult to lay because of their slightly uneven thickness. The window seen to the left of the dresser throws light into the internal corridor.

ABOVE This theatrical, dark space has walls painted in glossy Farrow & Ball Mahogany to eye level, and is hung with framed official notices from Hastings council dating from the mid-19th century. A door at the end to the right opens into the entrance hall, a door on the left into the dining room. Ahead are original fitted cupboards.

'You could accuse me of being an ego-maniac,' he comments, cheerfully, 'but if you can't live with your own work you probably shouldn't expect other people to want to.'

The most striking use of colour is the gloss Mahogany in the windowless central passage that separates the 17th-century house from the 18th-century additions at the back. This dark, slightly mysterious space with rows of doors on either side and original fitted cupboards is glamorized by the reflective dusky aubergine paintwork, against which a collection of framed official notices issued in Hastings in the mid-19th century looks all the more

graphic. These were a present from Andrew to Richard and make interesting reading, for example the 'Proclamation for a day of solemn fast, humiliation and prayer' from Queen Victoria to 'tender the favour of Almighty God' for 'the just and necessary War', or a petition against income tax or the announcement of a 'gale and floods relief fund'. So much for progress.

And so the interior of the house is finished. But now the couple are turning their attentions to outside, and relocating the drive to make the most of arriving in front of that stunning view. Nearly perfect, and certainly a house worth stalking.

ABOVE The spare bedroom features a fabric-covered four-poster bed hung with Ersari, and curtains and a footstool covered in a vibrant paisley Amasura, all No. 9 Thompson by Jim Thompson.

LEFT The main bedroom opens through a wide arch into a bathroom that extends above the front porch. The bathtub is carefully positioned to maximize the view. Richard encrusted plain wall lights from John Lewis with shells, and they are now known as 'the mermaid's bras'. The curtains are Jim's Garden and the screen is Phuwen, both No. 9 Thompson by Jim Thompson.

RIGHT A second spare bedroom has a glamorous half-tester bed and opens into a bathroom centred by a huge cast-iron bathtub in bright mint green that was already in the house and which Richard and Andrew managed to match with a similarly bright green vintage lavatory and washbasin.

TRADITIONAL FARMHOUSE
elements of style

• TABLE   A kitchen table, its wooden top marked by years of hearty breakfasts and family suppers, is the centre of operations in a farmhouse. Warm in winter, thanks to the regulation Aga, it is a place for doing homework, reading the Sunday papers, paying the bills and writing letters, as well as providing an extra kitchen work surface for rolling out pastry and kneading dough. Both new and antique versions tend to be expensive. Maggie Hadfield economized by using elm planks from a tree that died on her land, sawn and jointed by a carpenter, and resting on trestles. It is the top of the table you notice, not the legs.

• DRESSER   The next essential for the traditional farmhouse kitchen is a dresser. Good antique kitchen dressers, like good antique kitchen tables, cost a small fortune. But this is a piece of furniture that can be happily married; a 'marriage' being antiques-dealer-speak for a piece of furniture that is made up from other pieces. The shelves are a reasonably easy DIY task, but the base is more complicated if you want drawers. A junky old sideboard, with shelves sitting on it or fixed to the wall above it, unified with a good old-fashioned kitchen paint colour, such as Farrow & Ball's Mouse's Back, works very nicely.

• FOUR-POSTER   Along with the table, the dresser and the inescapable Aga, a four-poster bed is another icon of traditional farmhouse style. Again, rigging up your own is not as impossible a task as you might imagine, although basic wood-working skills are essential. Four-posters in some of the grandest interiors are often nothing more than a good pair of posts, joined to a modern framework and covered in fabric. Maggie Hadfield's half-tester, which is the next best thing to a full four-poster, is made from a section of old panelling to which a canopy has been attached. If you construct a four-poster around a divan box-spring bed base (making sure the divan itself is high enough to look authentic), the framework need not be structural, part of it can be attached to the wall and most of it can be disguised by the bed's hangings, as it is in Richard Smith and Andrew Blackman's spare bedroom.

• WALLS   In Lori Gibson's spare bedroom, a wide wallpaper border of roses has been applied in vertical stripes on a plain, painted wall to charming effect, a decorating trick famously used by John Fowler in the main bedroom of his country cottage, The Hunting Lodge.

• COLLECTIONS   Doris Urquhart is an inveterate, if extremely discerning, collector and her house is proof of her belief that quantity matters as much as quality when it comes to making a decorative statement. Instead of a single piece of creamware, she has a cupboard full. Instead of a single milliner's head, she has a row of three. She has a bowl of apple-shaped money boxes, a stack of Victorian bread boards and a sheaf of horn-handled carving knives. Easier to emulate is her collection of single candlesticks – always more affordable than pairs. Grouped at one end of her dining table, they make a handsome display and look even better when the candles are lit for evening entertaining.

Now to the pleasant pasture dells,
Where hay from closes sweetly smells,
Adown the pathway's narrow lane
The milking maiden hies again

JOHN CLARE (1793–1864)

FRESH
FARMHOUSE

LIGHT, PRETTY AND FRESH AS A BANK OF
PRIMROSES, OR A WOOD WASHED WITH
BLUEBELLS, HERE ARE ROOMS THAT SEEM TO
BRING THE GARDEN AND THE COUNTRYSIDE
INDOORS. ROSEBUDS GARLAND WALLS, POSIES
SCATTER CURTAINS AND BOUQUETS BLOSSOM
ON CUSHIONS AND IN PAINTINGS. THE FEEL IS
FEMININE AND INFORMAL, MORE MILKMAIDS AND
SUNBONNETS THAN PRIZE BULLS AND BOILER-
SUITS, AND THE COMBINATION OF FADED, FLORAL
FABRICS, GENTLE COLOURS THAT REFLECT AND
ENHANCE THE DAYLIGHT AND SIMPLE,
UNPRETENTIOUS FURNISHINGS GIVE THESE
FARMHOUSE INTERIORS AN IRRESISTIBLE CHARM.

VINTAGE VALUE

Holly and Philip Keeling's first priority was to find a house with space for their two boys. 'We were living in a town not far from the hospital where Phil works as a cardiologist, but we only had a small garden and the boys were seven and four and bursting with energy,' remembers Holly. 'We had seen this house a year before, and had been put off because it needed so much work. But it came with nine acres of land, and I knew I could make it into our ideal family home, so when we sold in Totnes we made an offer and took the plunge.'

In lush, fertile countryside between Dartmoor and the south coast of Devon, the farm must once have been substantial and successful. The house is large and well-proportioned, probably enlarged at the beginning of the 19th century when a symmetrical façade of sash windows was added onto an older building, fronting high-ceilinged reception rooms and bedrooms either side of a central staircase, and leaving the rooms at the back of the house with an earlier, more rambling feel.

OPPOSITE The porch and the dormer windows are new, but the sash windows date back to the early 19th century, when the old farmhouse was extended and modernized. The house stands in 9 acres of garden, field and orchard where the three children can enjoy a swimming pool, a trampoline, a swing and a zip line.

OPPOSITE CENTRE LEFT A lean-to piggery at the back of the house has been converted to make a studio where Holly makes her three-dimensional clay cards and pictures.

ABOVE and OPPOSITE BELOW LEFT The barn opposite the house is Holly's shop, stocked with vintage and antique pieces that Holly buys locally at auctions and fairs, including vintage fabrics, some of which she uses to make cushions, such as this one propped on a window seat.

LEFT At the back of the house, which is older, the ceilings are lower and there is a more cottagey feel. The door under the stairs in this inner hall leads down to the cellars, and shoes are stored in a vintage wire rack. The architectural fanlight standing on the rack has been fitted with mirror glass.

BELOW LEFT The kitchen is at the back of the house and has French doors onto a sunny terrace. Another door opens from the kitchen into the informal living room at the front of the house. The plain, panelled kitchen units were made by Barnes of Ashburton to Holly's design and the open shelves display some of her vintage storage jars.

OPPOSITE The Aga was already installed in the alcove of the original farmhouse kitchen fireplace.

The house was gutted but not finished before they moved, and they had to wash the dishes in the garden for the first few weeks until the kitchen was plumbed in. Holly kept as many original features as possible as well as the Aga, which was already installed in the wide alcove of the original kitchen fireplace, but photographs of the interior as they found it show how thoroughgoing her restoration and redecoration were. Rooms that were a mishmash of cheap fittings, and ill-thought-out wiring, are now light, bright and rational with pale paint colours and pretty, flowered fabrics. Furnishings are antique and vintage and include unusual finds, like the cupboard lined with rusting wire cubbyholes that Holly uses to store shoes in the back hall, or the little Parian ware dog under a dome that sits on the living room mantelpiece.

What is not immediately apparent is just how economically Holly has achieved all this charm. She is a familiar face at local auctions, and often gets up early at weekends to catch the best buys at car boot fairs. Almost all her furniture, pictures and decorative pieces were bought cheaply and within a short drive of her front door. In the living room that adjoins the kitchen, the sofa was from Totnes market, the table behind it and the watercolour of Babbacombe Bay above the fireplace from Rendells auction rooms. In the drawing room on the opposite side of the hall, there are two little oil paintings she found in a charity shop, and the chandelier was from Totnes market.

It is the same story throughout. Painted furniture bought for a song, a Victorian doll's house spotted at a boot fair. The bed in a spare bedroom is a copy made

by a carpenter of one found in a skip. Holly has a distinctive style, feminine and fashionable, and has long been in demand among friends and acquaintances for help with interior design and sourcing. More recently she has turned her talent and eye for a bargain into a successful career. Although the principal barns that once belonged to the house have been converted to make a separate house next door, Holly has turned two farm buildings into a shop selling antiques and decorative items, and a range of furnishing fabrics, meaning she can offer a full interior design service from home. She also works as a stylist, and when Tesco asked if she could style a food shoot, she was able to find the pine table and baskets from her own stock.

At the back of the house, in a lean-to that once housed pigs and is now a sunny studio with a wall of windows, Holly also works on other creative projects, such as the cards and pictures she crafts from clay.

ABOVE At the front of the house are two elegant reception rooms on either side of the staircase. Connecting with the kitchen, this is the less formal of the two rooms where the family gather together and watch television.

RIGHT The drawing room on the other side of the staircase is furnished with antiques and a chandelier bought at Totnes market.

OPPOSITE Across the hall from the kitchen is a room that was once used as a sheep pen and which is now Holly's office, where she works at an old metal desk set against a wall papered in her favourite Cole's Hummingbirds wallpaper. Here, as in the kitchen, she laid new limestone flooring where there would once have been flagstones.

THIS PAGE and RIGHT This first floor bedroom with connecting bathroom is elegantly furnished with painted and gilded antique furnishings in the French style in a sophisticated scheme of greys and mauves. The effect is luxurious and expensive-looking, but Holly insists it was achieved on a shoestring. The cover on the bed, for example, is an inexpensive printed Indian cotton bedspread.

OPPOSITE All three children have their own bedrooms on the first floor, while the top floor attic has been converted to make a suite of bedroom, dressing room and bathroom for Holly and Phil. In Charlotte's bedroom, an old pine sleigh bed fits perfectly into the alcove behind the door where the wall has been papered in Floral Trail by GP & J Baker. Appropriately enough, there is an old-fashioned toy farm under Charlotte's bed that she has peopled with models of the animals that provided a living for the farmers who worked here. This bedroom, like her brother Ben's, once housed Polish farm labourers.

BELOW and RIGHT The staircase was installed in the 19th century when the house was enlarged and aggrandized. Holly has carpeted it with a traditional stair runner from Roger Oates held in place by metal stair rods. At the top of the stairs is this bathroom, which Holly has painted in two shades of paint from Farrow & Ball, Lime White on the matchboarding and Blue Gray on the cupboard. The bath mat, mirror, stool and child's chair are all car boot fair and antiques market finds.

Next door, sheep used to be kept in her office, now fresh and attractively decorated with a wall of her favourite Cole's Hummingbirds wallpaper. It is hard to imagine that this immaculate house was once a workplace thick with the scent and sound of animals, and all the mess and muck that goes with them.

Outside, there are more telling clues to the building's agricultural past. If you climb the slope directly behind the house, you can look down and see exactly how the land and buildings once related as farm and farmyard. The orchard remains with its neat rows of gnarled apple trees, while a deep pit above the house has been turned into a swimming pool, the trampoline sits on top of a mound that is now neatly terraced and an adjacent field has wide paths mown through the long summer grasses, making perfect tracks for go-carting. Ben, now 13, and Louis, who is 10, have plenty of space in which to burn off energy, while their younger sister Charlotte, aged five, can have a lovely time being girly with her mother.

ABOVE To the right of the front door is the older part of the house, which probably dates back to the 17th century. This room was the playroom, but now that Bill and Becca's boys have grown out of it, it has become a pretty living room. The papier-mâché deer's head over the fireplace is by Emily Warren and the vintage lampshade was bought by Becca for £7.

OPPOSITE LEFT Becca collects flower paintings, which she always hangs unframed. In the kitchen the colours of the painted roses are picked up by the pink and blue of the vintage enamel pots and kettle.

OPPOSITE RIGHT The house has symmetrical Georgian façades that disguise the fact that part of it is much earlier. On this side, three drawing room windows overlook lawns, while on the opposite side of the house there is Bill's vegetable garden.

Bill is a big name in Lewes. His eponymous store, a grocery, café and restaurant, is thrumming with music and conversation from the minute it opens for breakfast. His name is printed on the red T-shirts of staff and on the cardboard takeaway cups, and shelves are lined with his signature, which bounds across the carefully aligned labels on jars of chutney, jam, marmalade and lemon curd, and on bottles of juice and beer. There is even a stack of Bill's cookbooks. So it is little wonder that his wife Becca says she is generally known as 'Bill's wife'.

A FLORAL FEAST

Bill and Becca Collison have known each other since she was a teenager and he was in his early twenties and would throw her an apple on her way to school as she walked past his first grocer's shop. Later she worked there as a Saturday girl, and when she came back from university in London, they married. Even in those early days, Bill was renowned for his gorgeous displays of fruit and vegetables. The shop moved to bigger premises, and with Becca taking charge of 'dry goods', all the office work and the payroll, they extended its stock, then added a café and a few years later opened another store in Brighton. More recently, thanks to the help of outside investors, Bill's stores have appeared in Covent Garden and Reading with more planned, and probably already open by the time you read this book.

THIS PAGE and OPPOSITE The drawing room, which stretches from the front to the back of the house and has four sash windows plus French windows, was originally two rooms. Becca has furnished it with second-hand and antique chairs and sofas bought at local auctions, piled with cushions made from vintage fabrics and grouped around the two fireplaces at either end of the room. Curtains are in a lustrous silk and the 18th-century portrait to the right of the window was a present to Becca from Bill.

'Bill makes everything look pretty,' says Becca, standing in the drawing room of their house on the edge of a village a ten-minute drive from the town where it all began. She is talking about the stores, where it is Bill who sees that glossy peppers are mounded in huge colanders and shiny tomatoes in enamel buckets, and that the carrot cake is spiked with sprigs of rosemary and the chocolate délice tiled with curved roundels of

orange. But the look inside the house is Becca's responsibility, and is ample evidence that she too has a talent for arranging and decorating, and an eye for colour and style.

Until 2004, when they moved out of town, Bill and Becca lived in a cottage an apple's throw from the shop. In 2000, they were temporarily made homeless by the floods that turned the streets of Lewes into rivers, but it wasn't until they were expecting a

third child that they decided they needed more bedrooms and a big garden. Becca says she instantly fell in love with this house, and was devastated when they lost it to a higher bid. 'After that we looked at what felt like 50 million other houses, but I still desperately wanted this one. So I phoned the estate agent to see how the sale was going and – guess what – it had all fallen through. At which point we snapped it up.'

Becca's determination is entirely understandable. The house is understated, English perfection, built in the soft, rosy brick typical of this part of Sussex, standing square and symmetrical with sash windows and an arched front door frilled by pink summer roses. Brick paths worn into gentle dips and humps wend their way around the house and up to the front door between beds of lavender, and the lawn slopes away to an edging of trees.

LEFT and ABOVE The old bakehouse, with its capacious brick bread oven, was originally a separate building but has been annexed to the kitchen to make a welcoming and spacious dining and sitting area. Leather chairs, bought at Ardingly antiques fair, are placed around the wide table that is covered in a tablecloth from Cabbages and Roses. A side table and wall shelves hold just some of Becca's large collection of flowery cups, saucers and plates, which are always used for special occasions, such as Easter tea.

On the other side of the track that leads off the road to the house, the original oast house has been converted into two houses where the farmer and his daughter now live. Other farm buildings have been converted to make holiday cottages. An old barn has become Bill and Becca's garage, and they have annexed the original bakehouse at the back of the house to make a dining and sitting room that opens from the kitchen.

Despite living in a male-dominated household, Becca has given the interior a gentle, feminine prettiness (while leaving the boys and their bedrooms

LEFT The blinds in the elegant family bathroom are made from material that Becca found in a skip after the floods in Lewes, and the glass-fronted armoire holds some of the vintage fabrics she uses to make cushions.

BELOW This tiny spare bedroom is known as the 'princess bedroom' in honour of its painted and gilded French furnishings, all bought at auction and antiques fairs.

OPPOSITE The only fabric in this pretty bedroom that is not vintage is the curtains, which are a faded floral linen from Cabbages and Roses.

to themselves). The drawing room, which has windows on three sides looking out over the gardens, has walls in a pale blue-green and the curtains are a lustrous, rustling eau-de-nil silk. She loves the soft, faded colours of antique and vintage textiles, and the sofas and armchairs are piled high with cushions cut from old curtains. Two big antique rugs are laid over the floorboards, there are peonies and delphiniums in a jug and propped on antique desks and hung on the wall are some of her collection of unframed flower paintings.

'I don't feel I have any particular style,' she says modestly, 'but there are certain things I like and will always buy – old, floral fabrics and eiderdowns, pretty antique china, and flower paintings – but only if they are not expensive. I go to auctions and car boot fairs, which is where almost everything in this house came from.' And just as Becca appreciates Bill's aesthetic – she calls him 'an artist with fruit and vegetables' – so he is happy to allow her taste to prevail at home, often buying her things he knows that she will like, such as the little linen-covered sofa at the dining end of the kitchen, and the portrait of a lady that hangs in the smaller sitting room. There has only been one recent tussle, over a faded chintz lampshade that Becca bought for a few pounds and loves but which is a step too far in the direction of shabby and away from chic for Bill. Initially they compromised on having it in use for a week, and putting it away for a week in turn. But the lampshade is there today, and it was there last week and it may still be there now.

OPPOSITE ABOVE and BELOW LEFT The granary, at right angles to the house, has been converted into a two-storey studio where Patricia Low makes her exquisite coil pots, examples of which are displayed on a shelf next to the wood-burning stove.

OPPOSITE ABOVE RIGHT Inside the house, a sofa covered in linen from Polish grain sacks stands against the oak screen wall of the living room.

OPPOSITE BELOW RIGHT The kitchen is housed in a single-storey extension at the back of the house.

RIGHT Seen through the branches of a catalpa tree, the original farmhouse rises behind a screen of box and holly.

BELOW RIGHT Samples of the glazes Patricia makes from ground oxides are pinned to the studio beams.

A POTTED HISTORY

For some years, potter Patricia Low took in lodgers to help make ends meet. 'One of the first was Georgina von Etzdorf – I am wearing one of her beautiful skirts today,' she smiles. 'For a while I was renting out every scrap of space. I even had to step over a mattress and through a curtain to get into my studio to work. People would always say they only needed to stay for a few weeks, and then would be here for at least three years. But they were usually so delightful and interesting that I didn't mind in the least.'

Patricia Low lives in a small, brick and flint farmhouse on a lane in a tiny Hampshire hamlet surrounded by cows and fields of wheat, their golden slopes framed by dark hedges. Sitting in her garden on a summer afternoon in the shade of an ageing catalpa tree, the only sound is birdsong, the clip, clip, clip of garden shears and the faint rumble of a distant tractor. Marcus, a friend who recently gave Patricia a present of a bicycle, has arrived to clean the windows. Anne, who helps with the house and garden once a week, is trimming the box hedge by the back door. Later in the afternoon the pair of barn owls, who have taken up residence in the barn that faces

LEFT The ground floor of the farmhouse consists of three rooms, including this surprisingly large central hall from which the dining room leads off to the right, and the living room to the left. 'It's a complete waste of space,' says Patricia, 'a folie de grandeur in a house this size.' The terracotta floor tiles were taken from a house next door that was due to be demolished.

RIGHT The room that is now the dining room was the original farmhouse kitchen and the huge fireplace has a bread oven to its left, so capacious that Patricia has opened it out to make a larder. The red lacquer grandfather clock was inherited from Patricia's grandmother.

the back of the house, float silently over the lawn to find food for their greedy chicks who sit hissing in hungry anticipation until they return. It seems hardly surprising if, having made themselves at home, the various lodgers found it difficult to leave.

Patricia's main studio, where she makes her large, exquisite pots, is at right angles to the farmhouse in a building that used to be a two-storey granary. More recently, she has finished converting an old cart house and stables to make a second studio with a kitchen and bathroom to which she can retreat when one of her daughters and three grandchildren come to stay, filling the bedrooms of the main house. Sometimes she invites friends to use this smaller studio as a country getaway, but the days of having to step over mattresses are long gone. Now there are lawns and neatly clipped trees between the various outbuildings where once there was concrete. The modern milking sheds have gone and instead there is a haze of lavender hedge and a deep herbaceous border lush with white Michaelmas daises, blue delphiniums, spires of hollyhocks in pink and palest yellow and the Gothic branches of thistles topped by the turbans of their small purple flowers. The hedges have thickened, the trees have matured and the contents of the house have settled into a comfortable certainty, as though they have always been in residence.

'It took two years of manual labour to make it habitable when we first moved in 30 years ago,' Patricia remembers. 'The tenant farmer had moved out, the house had been empty for five years and there were waist-high nettles surrounding it.' Working on a limited budget, Patricia says she turned into an expert scavenger. 'All the building materials were reclaimed

or found in skips. The terracotta floor tiles in the hall came from a house next door that was due to be demolished. I crawled through the hedge and back to get them. I love reusing things.'

The house has a symmetrical layout and few rooms but all are a good size, including the entrance hall, which is as big as the dining room to its right, and the sitting room to its left, so it feels spacious if compact. These three rooms complete the ground floor with a kitchen in a single-storey

ABOVE On a side table beneath the staircase in the hall is one of Patricia's large pots featuring a wild boar. She made sketches for it from life and says that pigs of all types love being drawn: 'They start posing, and rolling around.' Another of her pots decorated with an intricate repeat of pineapple motifs holds roses from the garden.

ABOVE LEFT and RIGHT The kitchen is in a single-storey extension that was once the scullery. China mugs and teapots on the shelves to the left of the plate rack are designs by Patricia's daughter Charlie, who also made the decorated tiles. Charlie and her husband now own Branksome Pottery and Patricia takes great pride in using their products, including the mugs seen here. The vase is by Joanna Still, the potter who first inspired Patricia to turn from painting on paper and canvas to painting on pots.

RIGHT The cushion on the chaise longue in the living room and the curtains are both antique. 'All the curtains in the house are second-hand,' says Patricia, 'which is why all of them are much too long for my cottagey windows. Some of the nicest were completely free, as they were going to be thrown away.'

extension that opens off the dining room. Upstairs, Patricia's bedroom occupies the space above the living room, and two further bedrooms and a bathroom sit above the hall and dining room. From the landing a door opens onto a steep wooden stair up to the attic, which has its own kitchen and bathroom dating from the days of lodgers.

Just like the materials, the furnishings are of the well-worn variety. All the curtains are old, which is why so many of them sit puddled on the floor,

having been made for much taller windows. All of them are beautiful, whether 19th-century floral, glazed chintz or more sumptuous brocade, and several pairs were completely free, rescued by Patricia's enthusiasm. 'I am mad about old textiles,' she says. The charming rosebud stripe wallpaper in Patricia's bedroom is as old as some of the curtains and quite rubbed away in places. It stops two-thirds of the way around the room, where once there was a corridor that led to an ancient lavatory in what is now a corner of her bedroom.

ABOVE LEFT The charming rosebud stripe wallpaper and wallpaper border in Patricia's bedroom were there when she bought the house 30 years ago and probably date back much further. The iron bedstead is Victorian.

Pretty much the only new things in the house are the prints, paintings and pots by artist friends, and the Branksome china in its original 1950s pastel glazes and elegant, pleasing shapes. Tea and coffee is served in Branksome mugs, their plain, neutral exteriors in delightful contrast with the pearly mauves, primrose yellows and periwinkle blues of their inner surfaces, and lunch comes on pale celadon green Branksome plates. Patricia is prouder of her Branksome china than she is of her own work, examples of which she sometimes brings in from the studio to live with,

ABOVE All the textiles are antique or vintage, including the lace-trimmed sheets and pillowcases and the bedspread that forms a valance. A vintage rug is folded on the chair and a Victorian paisley shawl on the old pine trunk at the foot of the bed.

before they get snapped up in her next exhibition. 'Branksome was bought by my daughter Charlie and her husband Philip Johnson,' she explains. Unlike the Branksome pieces, which are designed for everyday use, Patricia's pots are one-off works of art, decorated with extraordinarily mobile and detailed paintings of animals, from pet lurchers to wild boar, each one the product of months of painstaking drawing and redrawing. Very occasionally one collapses in the kiln. 'I just put the pieces in a cardboard box and get on with the next one,' says Patricia.

ABOVE Like the bedroom wallpaper, the roll-top bathtub was already in situ and 'the only modern thing in the whole house,' says Patricia. The old-fashioned bathroom scales probably date from a similar era and were bought from a friend's junkyard. While furnishings and textiles are almost all antique, the house is full of paintings, prints and pots by Patricia's friends, including some by Patricia herself, like this portrait of her daughter Siobhan as a baby. The landscape with straw bales, painted at first light, is by Terry Raybold.

RIGHT The third bedroom on the first floor of the house is furnished with an antique sleigh bed that Patricia bartered for one of her pots, and more antique textiles. The chair has two layers of old fabric; its original loose cover and another slip cover, which Patricia says is 'incredibly torn and tatty but very pretty'.

OPPOSITE ABOVE LEFT and
THIS PAGE FAR RIGHT and
BELOW Ursula and Toby Falconer
bought their house at a nail-biting
auction. It was advertised as a
'traditional, Cotswold country
farmhouse for improvement' and had
not been lived in for ten years. One of
Ursula and Toby's many improvements,
was to reinstate sash windows.

RIGHT Toby found the library
fireplace lying in a field covered in ivy.

OPPOSITE ABOVE CENTRE
The barn next to the house, where the
farmer once kept calves and chickens,
has been converted to make a home
for Ursula's mother.

OPPOSITE ABOVE RIGHT and
BELOW The kitchen is in a former
outbuilding attached to the main
house and was originally the dairy.
The dresser, which stretches along one
wall, has shelf brackets cut in the shape
of silhouette portraits of Ursula and her
three children. Toby's silhouette is
painted on the side of the base.

AUCTION HOUSE

*Twenty years ago, Ursula and Toby Falconer were living in the house
immortalized by Laurie Lee as the 'big house' belonging to the Squire in*
Cider With Rosie. *What could be lovelier, except that the house had been
divided into two and their portion was at the back. 'I longed for sunlight,'
Ursula explains. But period Cotswold houses, bathed in golden sunlight,
are not so easy to come by on a limited budget. 'Nor did I want to pay for
someone else's expensive kitchen and have to rip it out,' Ursula continues,
'so we were looking for something south-facing, unspoilt and unrestored,
and there was nothing we could afford.'*

When Ursula saw an advertisement for a farmhouse being sold at auction
on the edge of a nearby village, she was instantly intrigued. 'I knew the
valley where the house must be. I was so excited that I got up incredibly
early the next morning and tore down to have a look. On the lane, I met
the lovely farmer who part-owned the farmhouse, and he asked me to help
him with the cows. So I put my boots on and gave him a hand. He lived in
a cottage, but the farmhouse itself, which he and his brother had inherited,
hadn't been occupied for ten years and there were fertilizer sacks pinned up
in some of the windows where the glass was missing. When I got home I
realized I had left my shoes behind when I put on my boots, so I had to

LEFT and ABOVE The flagged floor in the kitchen sloped into a gully, now ironed out, where the water that cooled the milk for cheese making, drained away. The room faces south and is made lighter and brighter due to the ceiling and ceiling beams having been painted white. The door to the right of the chimney breast opens into the larder (above), which has traditional slate shelving.

RIGHT The window above the sink looks into the back hall, a lean-to extension added later. The door to the right of the sink opens onto a staircase that leads directly up to the main bedroom. It still has its old dark blue-green paint, a colour matched exactly by the cupboards that form the base of the kitchen dresser, which also retain their original paintwork.

call the farmer to ask if I could come back to collect them, and he said that it was a very lucky sign if you had to return somewhere you had just visited.'

The shoes were the first good omen, the second was the date of the auction, which fell on Ursula's birthday. 'When Toby and I viewed the house it was crawling with hundreds of people,' she remembers, 'and there was huge interest in it at the auction. But we kept on bidding and it turned into a battle between us and a beautiful young couple with a vintage car. When the hammer finally came down and we had bought it, we were terrified but also elated. A few months later, I found I was pregnant.'

Ursula's twins, Augusta and Ned, were born while their parents were in the midst of a major restoration project. The farmhouse is in a particularly lovely location at the end of its own private road with rolling fields in front and woods cloaking the distant hills. But photographs dating from just after they bought it, showing it with blank windows, a semi-derelict extension and an ugly concrete barn, reveal just how hard they have worked on its transformation.

The main part of the house is 18th century but had lost all its original windows, fireplaces and much of its period charm. The ground floor of the extension had been used as a dairy where a

local cheese of some repute was made. The room above, now their bedroom, was lined with wooden shelving for storing the cheeses. 'There was an ancient truckle of cheese still hanging from a beam, but the farmer was so embarrassed when we told him about it that he whisked it away,' laughs Ursula.

Perhaps the Falconers would not have been courageous enough to take on the restoration had they not both been so ideally qualified for the job. Ursula, who trained in history of art, is an all-round artist-craftsman who paints and draws, as well as being skilled at gilding and making decorative plasterwork. Toby Falconer is an architect who specializes in the conservation (and

alteration where necessary) of historic houses and churches. Between them, they shared the talent, knowledge and visual acuity to tease out the beauty from these neglected buildings, saving everything worth preserving, replacing the anachronistic and inappropriate and adding their own inventions.

Sash windows took the place of fertilizer sacks, they bought reclaimed stone tiles to clad the roof of the extension, excavated an original inglenook with alcove seating in the room that is now the drawing room, replaced chimneypieces, mended floorboards, planted a yew hedge, medlar and quince trees and demolished the ugly barn and planted a walled garden where it stood.

THIS PICTURE The drawing room is one of two front rooms in the 18th-century farmhouse and has an inglenook fireplace opposite the door to the hall. This is so capacious that it incorporates alcove seats on either side, ideal for use on wintry evenings, each with its own little shelf – 'one for his pint, one for her port and lemon,' jokes Ursula. Toby designed the bay window in Arts and Crafts style with leaded lights and a deep window seat.

THIS PICTURE When Ursula and Toby bought the house, this north-facing room at the back of the house was being used as the kitchen. After they moved the kitchen into the old dairy at the front of the house, it became an informal sitting room and playroom, and even though two of their children have now left school, Ursula and Toby still call it the nursery.

OPPOSITE ABOVE Small oil paintings by Ursula and Toby's daughter, Augusta, are propped on the mantelpiece.

'We did it piecemeal by necessity,' explains Ursula, 'and eventually we moved the kitchen from the back of the house into the old dairy, which faces south, and I got my sunshine.'

The Falconers' decorative additions to the house are so subtle it is a surprise to find they are not period features. Ursula has added a charming plaster frieze in the hall, taken from a mould by Arts and Crafts architect Norman Jewson, that has a distinctly 17th-century feel. The fitted dresser in the kitchen is even more deceptive. Far from being an old retainer, it is an ingenious parvenu. The cupboard fronts, bought from a local reclamation yard, have weather-beaten paintwork that happens to match the rubbed peacock blue of a door in the same room; the worn wooden top is an old railway bench bought from a different reclamation yard at a different time; the wall shelves above are new and were cut with a band-saw to follow the silhouette portraits of each member of the family, including their third child, Algy, an added charm that only becomes apparent once pointed out.

The house came with enough land to keep a small flock of sheep, and there are plenty of outbuildings for storage. The barn nearest to the house is currently being converted to make a new home for Ursula's mother. As for the lovely farmer, he sold his cows but stayed in the cottage just down the lane.

ABOVE Toby and Ursula's bedroom is above the kitchen and when they bought the house was lined with wooden shelves that were used to store the cheeses made in the dairy downstairs. The bed has a simple canopy made from a length of embroidery by Chelsea Textiles.

LEFT Another length of Chelsea Textiles embroidered linen covers the entrance to a steep staircase that leads up to the attic in the pitch of the roof.

RIGHT Ursula decorated the spare bedroom 20 years ago and hasn't changed it since. The wallpaper is from Colefax and Fowler.

THIS PAGE The bathroom that adjoins the main bedroom retains its old planked ceiling and had been used as a storeroom before Ursula and Toby restored and converted it. Behind the bathtub, they have installed a tongue-and-groove partition with doors into two small dressing rooms, one each, with hanging space and shelving for clothes. The lavatory is disguised by a Victorian commode with a hinged seat.

FRESH FARMHOUSE
elements of style

• **FLORALS** This is a style of decorating that is pretty, relaxed and essentially feminine. Flowers are a key element, whether adorning fabrics, china and wallpaper or as the subject of paintings and prints. For informal charm, keep colours gentle and faded, and mix a selection of different floral designs in the same room, as Becca Collison does in her drawing room and spare bedroom. Areas of plain colour help to ensure that the effect is not too busy.

• **OLD CURTAINS** All the houses in this chapter use antique and vintage fabrics; Becca Collison cuts up second-hand curtains for cushions, Holly Keeling has made a roman blind from antique linen with a border of vintage toile and Ursula Falconer has an old Indian bedspread as a tablecloth in her kitchen. Patricia Low tops them all with exclusively antique and second-hand curtains, several pairs having been scavenged from boxes in a basement where they were awaiting disposal. Most of Patricia's grand, old curtains are far too big for her small farmhouse windows, but rather than cutting them up, she simply allows them to 'puddle' comfortably on the floor.

• **WALLPAPER** Different scales of wallpaper have radically different effects. Ursula Falconer has used a small yellow and white sprig in her spare bedroom, and a large-scale tree-of-life in her hall. In the bedroom the wallpaper is a background for the contents of the room, but in the hall the striking pattern is enough to decorate the space without the addition of pictures on the walls or furniture. In fact, the only items in the hall are three children's chairs.

• **UNFRAMED** Becca Collison collects paintings of flowers, many of which date from the first half of the last century. However, she prefers them unframed. This not only has the effect of making the paintings themselves look more simple and relaxed, and therefore more stylish and contemporary, it also makes them cheaper as she puts their various frames back into auction.

• **EIDERDOWNS** Fat feather eiderdowns, their contents held in place by stitched patterns, were both fashionable and essential warmth during the first half of the last century, when centrally heated bedrooms were still a rare luxury. Today we appreciate them for their old-fashioned decorative appeal and the nostalgic allure of their typically flowery or paisley fabrics. It is useful to know that they can be safely laundered on a delicate cycle, the trick being to tumble dry them with a couple of tennis balls, which helps to ensure that their feather filling remains evenly distributed and doesn't clump.

• **BED CANOPY** Ursula Falconer has made a simple and elegant bed canopy from a length of flower-sprigged, embroidered fabric by suspending it on a rod and wires against the wall behind her bed, and looping it up to a ceiling beam where it is pinned to form a gentle swag. Beams are not essential to achieve this effect, but they do make fixing the fabric to the ceiling much easier.

Happy the man whose wish and care
A few paternal acres bound,
Content to breathe his native air
In his own ground.

ALEXANDER POPE (1688–1744)

NO FRILLS
FARMHOUSE

THE FARMHOUSES IN THIS CHAPTER ARE NOT
MINIMAL IN THE MODERN SENSE, NOR ARE THEY
UNCOMFORTABLY AUSTERE, BUT THEY ALL
BENEFIT FROM AN AESTHETIC THAT BANISHES
THE EXTRANEOUS AND THE ILL-MATCHED.
AT FIRST GLANCE THEIR STYLES ARE VERY
DIFFERENT; ONE IS FILLED WITH CONTEMPORARY
FURNISHINGS, ONE WITH VINTAGE PIECES FROM
THE MID-20TH CENTURY, THE OTHER TWO A MIX
OF ANTIQUE AND SECOND-HAND FINDS. PARED
BACK, THESE ARE HOMES WHERE AS MUCH
IMPORTANCE IS GIVEN TO THE SPACE AND
BEAUTY OF THE SURROUNDING LAND. WHAT
LINKS THEIR INTERIORS IS MORE A QUESTION OF
WHAT THEY LACK: FUSS, FRILLS AND CLUTTER.

Eva Johnson is Swedish but has lived in England for most of her life. Having trained as a physiotherapist, she married an English academic, had four children, spent time living in Iran and Thailand and then settled near Cambridge where her husband Edward, a linguist, is still based. For more than 20 years now, Eva has lived in this red brick farmhouse surrounded by fields, with a view of an ancient church on one side and the moat of an Elizabethan manor house on the other. Roses ramble, gravel crunches and little pyramids of clipped yew march neatly along the edge of a curving lawn. It couldn't be more English. And yet inside the house, the light, the colours, the furnishings, the airy, informal, almost transient feel, as if contents and curtains could be lifted away in an afternoon without leaving a trace, are unmistakably Scandinavian.

SWEDISH LIGHT

OPPOSITE ABOVE Extensive outbuildings include an old piggery now used as a wood shed, a game larder with wire mesh windows and a Victorian hothouse.

OPPOSITE BELOW In the drawing room there is a spinet that Edward built from a kit and a lute propped against the wall behind the sofa.

BELOW Like so many very old buildings, the house has undergone several different periods of extension and alteration. From this side you can clearly see where the early 18th-century front half of the house with its sash windows was attached to the 16th-century house, the roof of which is taller. When they first bought the house, the two halves were beginning to separate and Eva says they hardly dared bang the front door in case large cracks appeared.

The style suits the house well. When they bought it, complete with its open-sided cart house, hay barn, stables, piggery, Victorian hothouse and potting sheds, the house was dilapidated and dour thanks to black floorboards and beams, its walls papered and painted in sombre colours. The oldest part of the house dates from the 15th century and was originally a row of three tiny cottages facing the churchyard. In the 16th century, the room that is now the kitchen and the bedrooms above were added and it probably became a single dwelling. At the beginning of the 18th century, the house was doubled in size when the two front reception rooms and entrance hall were built on behind a new façade. Later still, the windows of these rooms were extended to make three-sided bays.

'People assume that the house must have been the vicarage,' says Eva, 'but the vicar would have lived at the main house with the family. 'This was the farm for the estate, and it was separated and hidden from the house across the moat by a high brick wall. There was a huge, thatched tithe barn on the other side of our drive, which fell into disrepair and collapsed in the last century after the tenant farmer left.' Eva and Edward make good use of the remaining outbuildings, keeping

LEFT The slightly ascetic feel of the interiors with their pale colours and bare floorboards is relieved by the cosiness of fabrics such as the sheepskin rug and cashmere throw that soften this metal lounger by the fireplace in the dining room.

THIS PAGE The entrance hall has a particularly Scandinavian feel with its 18th-century Gustavian bench complete with original soft, grey paintwork. Even the hats are aesthetically pleasing and conform to the monochrome colour scheme. The door into the dining room is left open, as Eva likes a flow of light between rooms.

cars in the cart house, and using the stables as a workshop and the old hay barn as storage. When their daughters were married, this barn was transformed with garlands of flowers and hay-bale seating to make an enchantingly bucolic setting for the receptions.

The house still has the feel of a farmhouse. The big kitchen at the back opens onto a courtyard, on the other side of which is a game larder, and there is a pantry and rooms that may once have been a dairy and a bakehouse. Stripped back during a painstaking seven-year restoration, the older parts of the house now reveal their timber framework. In these early rooms, windows are smaller with leaded lights, while later rooms are lit by sash windows. Uniting the different styles and periods of architecture are wooden floorboards that run throughout the house, upstairs

ABOVE LEFT All the old outbuildings have found a new use, whether as storage, workshops or the venue for wedding receptions.

ABOVE CENTRE By inserting glazed panels into doors, Eva has ensured that the once dark house is well lit throughout, even in inner spaces like the staircase hall beyond the entrance hall.

ABOVE RIGHT Eva uses the shelved cupboard in the alcove to the left of the old kitchen range to store crockery – some old, some new – and has painted the walls blue.

FAR RIGHT There is a productive vegetable garden, and potted herbs sit on the kitchen windowsill.

OPPOSITE The dining room is furnished with the simple, graceful Swedish antique pieces that Eva inherited from her grandparents, all of them painted in the warm, gentle grey paint that characterizes Gustavian style. The bay windows in this room and the drawing room were added in the 19th century and here are fitted with invitingly deep, cushioned window seats. As elsewhere, the pine floorboards have been treated with lye, giving them a pale, silvery sheen.

and down, with only the occasional flat-weave rug and runner laid over them. And it is the floors more than any other internal feature that give the rooms their pared-back, pale Swedish beauty. 'I have a very strong feeling about floors,' says Eva. 'We had to sand off the black paint and then we treated all the old pine boards with lye, which is a traditional Scandinavian finish. The lye bleaches the wood, then you seal it with a vegetable oil, and maintain the finish with a special soap that contains coconut fat.'

All the floors and much of the woodwork, including beams, door surrounds, lintels, planked walls and even some furnishings, have been treated with lye. Recognizing a demand, Eva now imports and sells Scandinavian lye, and the finishing oil and soap, under the trade name Trip Trap. Her house is the ideal advertisement for its silvery good looks and durability. As a setting for the soft grey of the painted Gustavian dining table, chairs and sideboard, or the sleek lines of the Biedermeier sofa, all inherited from her grandparents, the bleached sheen of the wood has just the right restrained simplicity.

This restraint is carried through in the neutral colour scheme of the house, with walls painted in Farrow & Ball's soft distemper in Lime White.

ABOVE The bed is placed centrally in the main bedroom with a pine chest serving as a bedhead.

LEFT The bathroom is partitioned from the landing by a planked wall with glazing along the top, allowing extra light to filter through to the staircase. Here, the lye used on walls and flooring is both practical and good-looking, sealing the wood so that it does not soak up moisture. The bathtub itself sits on a slab of marble.

Aside from little bursts of pink and green afforded by the fresh flowers that decorate almost every room, blue is the only bright colour allowed to intrude. Early blue and white bowls are displayed on a shelf in the dining room, and there are blue doors and paintwork in the kitchen. 'I like to paint the inside of cupboards blue,' Eva reveals, opening a larder next to the kitchen range to show walls and shelving the colour of a summer sky.

The discipline of the colour palette is sustained in the furnishing fabrics, which are simple linens and plain or checked cottons verging on the frugal. Linen tea towels that fall short of the windowsill by several inches frame one of the kitchen windows, while a single tea towel pegged to a metal rail affords minimal privacy in the bathroom. The curtains in the main bedroom are unlined white cotton and not even wide enough to pull across the windows.

In this same room, Eva and Edward's bedroom, clothes are hung on pegs and the bed sits in the middle with a low chest behind it in place of a headboard, adding to the sense of impermanence created by the makeshift curtains and bare boards. It is almost ascetic, like a painting of an 18th-century cottage interior, doubtless why the style suits the house so well.

ABOVE LEFT Eva and Edward seem to have an unerring eye for composition and even their logs and garden tools are arranged in a pleasing manner.

ABOVE RIGHT Arriving at the farmhouse the drive passes the cart lodge, a long, open-sided beamed outbuilding that dates back to the 16th century. Eva and Edward use it as a garage for their cars but it also houses this old trailer, a reminder of how picturesque its contents once must have been when oxen and heavy horses were the farmer's equivalent of today's tractors.

LOCATION, LOCATION

Nick Ivins is a country man. He was born in Sussex, not far from where he lives now, and remembers watching commuters drive past as he walked to school and thinking 'I never want to do that'. His wife, Bella Pringle, has had to learn to be a country woman. 'I was brought up in South West London and when I met Nick I was living in an immaculate, minimal flat in Clapham and working for a publisher. If you had asked me, I would have said I never wanted to live in the country.'

At the time, Nick, who trained in land management at the Royal Agricultural College, Cirencester, was working as a photographer and travelling between Sussex and London – commuting, in fact, albeit to studios rather than an office. But he is a persuasive man, and when they married he managed to convince Bella that a tiny cottage in a Sussex village would be an ideal first home.

Sitting with Bella and Nick at their kitchen table in the farmhouse they bought six years ago, their two little girls Flora and Peggy sharing Nick's lap next to a bowl of garden vegetables and a basket of fresh eggs, the conversion from urban chick to country chic seems complete. Bella has even learned to keep bees, and will soon be collecting the honey, a task that she describes as a mad dash to get inside and shut the door before the burgled bees catch up with her. A new puppy is curled up on a beanbag, and a fluffy golden lurcher under the table. There are pigs, chickens and quail in the field just beyond the garden. 'The children have quail eggs in their school lunch boxes, dahling,' Nick quips, putting on a suitably privileged accent.

OPPOSITE TOP LEFT The ginger pig became famous in the village when he stole and drank a can of lager while Nick was mending the fence of his enclosure.

OPPOSITE CENTRE and BELOW LEFT and THIS PAGE, LEFT and ABOVE The pigs provide bacon, ham and sausages, the chickens provide eggs and the extensive vegetable garden yields a bountiful array of fruit and vegetables. There are also quail, whose eggs are a school lunch-box delicacy, and Bella has learned how to keep bees and has hives in the field beyond the vegetable garden.

OPPOSITE RIGHT On the landing at the top of the stairs, Nick's boots and shoes are stored in an old wooden shelving unit, while the glazed wall cupboard contains a mix of unrelated items, from reels and bobbins to preserving jars and old photographs.

What with them all being so good-looking, the farm and its surrounding land being so picturesque and the interior of the house so relaxed and stylish, it is a bit like walking into an advertisement for a posh supermarket. This is not without its benefits, and nor is it accidental. One of the ways they 'sweat the asset', as Nick humorously puts it, is by renting the house, garden, fields and woodland out as a location for film and photography. Recently, a crew of 65 moved in to film an advertisement for L'Oreal starring Rachel Weisz. 'The village was agog,' says Nick, 'although we were all a bit disappointed that Daniel Craig didn't pay us a visit. I can, however, offer you a seat on the very sofa where Rachel Weisz rested between scenes,' he laughs, adding, 'Of course, all our animals are chosen entirely for their photogenic qualities.' And it is true that the new whippet puppy is in a particularly desirable shade of velvety slate-grey.

Buying the farmhouse was a gamble. It was run-down, overgrown and generally in very bad shape, yet it was also beyond their means. They first tried to buy it with a sealed bid but were unsuccessful and so took their cottage off the market. Then someone knocked on the door and asked if they were still selling, and Bella, who according to Nick is 'a bit of a terrier', phoned up to see if the deal on the farmhouse had gone through.

OPPOSITE FAR LEFT The kitchen runs along the back of the house and was added in the early 1800s to an older house, of which this brick was once the outside wall. The older part of the house has two rooms either side of the staircase. This door from the kitchen opens into one of these rooms, which is used as a living room.

OPPOSITE BELOW LEFT Looking back from the same living room, where walls are painted in Farrow & Ball's Down Pipe, into the kitchen.

THIS PAGE and **OPPOSITE ABOVE RIGHT** The room on the other side of the staircase is grandly called 'the library', and is furnished with a battered Regency sofa.

OPPOSITE and THIS PAGE
The kitchen was once two rooms, now
opened up, and has been given extra
light thanks to the addition of French
doors at the end of the room. The only
part of the kitchen that is fitted is the
sink. The rest of the furnishings are
antique cupboards, tables and chests,
unified by white paint.

It turned out it hadn't, and Bella negotiated a new price for the farmhouse on the phone while driving. Nick says he listened from the passenger seat 'with my head in my hands', but readily admits in retrospect that it was entirely the right decision.

They moved in when Flora was still a baby. Their photograph album recording those early days in the house shows appealing images of Bella looking pretty in Wellington boots cooking on a tagine in the courtyard, of Nick slumped comically in a wheelbarrow and of the house starting to emerge from the surrounding undergrowth. 'We cleared at least four skip-loads of scrap metal and broken glass, and Flora had a toy kitchen before Bella had a real one,' says Nick. 'And we couldn't even afford a decent wheelbarrow. We had to do everything ourselves, and it was incredibly hard work and went on being incredibly hard work for much too long.' Proof that what makes a beautiful image is not always a beautiful experience.

Fortunately, although the land was in terrible shape, the house was structurally sound. 'Our main aim was to try to let in more light,' says Bella. The kitchen spans the back of the house and there are two rooms and a hall at the front with the stairs between. 'We put glass in the front door to light the hall and stairs, and a French door at one end of the kitchen. We also put in a door from the library to the kitchen so that all the rooms lead one into the other and round again.'

ABOVE In this bedroom, the beams have been left unpainted. The apricot gloss paint on the door and the window has also been left just as Nick and Bella found it. The French painted mirror adds a dash of glamour.

OPPOSITE ABOVE RIGHT Looking from the bedroom pictured above across the landing into Bella and Nick's bedroom, where instead they have painted the beams white.

OPPOSITE ABOVE and BELOW LEFT In Nick and Bella's bedroom the fitted cupboards in alcoves on either side of the fireplace are original, and the Suffolk Punch horse silhouette, bought by Bella in a Richmond antiques shop, is cut out of plywood and was possibly made as a pub sign.

Aside from painting and furnishing the rooms with an attractive mix of artistically shabby antiques and unusual finds such as the cut-out plywood Suffolk Punch horse on a bedroom wall, they have left well alone.

Nick now works as a wedding photographer and is much in demand at tasteful nuptials from the Home Counties to Lake Geneva. But he is most at home out in his gardens and fields, and thinks nothing of gutting a pheasant, carving up a deer for venison or cooking the squirrels, rabbits and pigeons that Bunny the lurcher regularly catches and kills. Meanwhile, Bella looks after the locations side of the business, working from an office in the old granary opposite the house. She also caters if required, organizes accommodation and transport and makes people welcome.

Nick thinks the farm must have been quite successful in the 1800s when the house was extended to its current size, but more recently the farmers who lived here and reared cows for beef all had other jobs in order to make ends meet. 'I like to think we are keeping the farming side of things going a bit,' he says, 'even if only in a rather Marie Antoinette-ish way.'

OPPOSITE TOP LEFT Buzz the golden labrador poses in the Gothic arched doorway of the back hall.

OPPOSITE BELOW LEFT The house is bisected by a traditional cross passage that leads from the front door to the back of the house.

OPPOSITE RIGHT Three steps down from the kitchen is the living and dining area.

RIGHT Vintage chairs and sofas, bought from advertisements in the local paper, stand on an IKEA rug in front of the huge living room fireplace.

BELOW and FAR RIGHT Buzz poses again in the doorway of the old threshing barn that now houses a trampoline, and bounds across the grass outside his kennel.

FASHIONING THE PAST

The owners of this West Country farmhouse are a fashion editor and a writer, and had you met them ten years ago you would have thought them the very last people you could imagine happily settled at the end of a bumpy track surrounded by buttercups and sheep. Five miles from the nearest shop, with distant views of fields and hills, their ancient farmhouse is about as far removed from the gloss of Vogue House and the chatter of The Groucho Club as a walking boot from a Louboutin slingback.

'David was a diehard Notting Hiller,' Maddie smiles, 'and, although I was brought up in the country, I couldn't wait to get to London as a teenager. When we first got married we lived in a flat in Clapham, but then Dan was born and everything changed. As soon as he was mobile, he could empty the kitchen cupboards within five minutes, and I got so bored with the walk to the park. David was the first to suggest we should move out of London. I had decided not to go back to work after maternity leave and thought that

if I was going to make one big change I might as well make another. We wanted real countryside, not Home Counties commuter belt, so we came down here and rented a house for three months as an experiment. For the first time Dan had all the space he needed.'

Seven years later they have two children, both thriving at the local school, a dog, and 'a ridiculous quantity of Wellington boots'. Having house-hunted for nearly three years while continuing to rent, Maddie says they knew immediately they had found what they wanted when a friend tipped them off that this house was for sale. 'My dream was a house in the middle of a field, and this was as close as you could get.'

The house had been lived in by the same farmer for 50 years but was no longer being run as a farm. The outbuildings were falling down, the vegetable garden was a jungle of brambles and the house was crammed with heavy, dark furniture. Maddie is modest about her skills as an interior designer, but after three years

OPPOSITE The kitchen is a later extension built onto the back of the original farmhouse, but it still has the flagged floors that characterize the older downstairs rooms. The chairs are vintage Ercol and the mugs, cups and teapot are Branksome china.

THIS PAGE The vintage Ercol armchair and table were both bought locally, but the Ercol chairs around the dining table are new from Margaret Howell. Maddie has left some of the walls unplastered because she likes the contrast of textures between the plaster and the bare brick and wood. The door is open onto the cross passage where light floods in from the front door.

'practising living in the country', she had firm ideas about how to organize the space. 'In London we hardly had people round for dinner, but once we moved we had endless friends and their children to stay, so good guest accommodation was important. In London I had a winter coat and a summer coat, but in the country you need a whole room where you can take off muddy boots and store the enormous variety of outerwear you suddenly find you need. And, since clutter makes me anxious and cross, I had to have really good storage, and that included a giant freezer so I wouldn't have to spend all my time driving miles to the shops.'

Once the interior had been stripped back to its essentials of stone and wood, and the lime plaster walls had been painted a uniform white, storage became the next priority. 'We were incredibly lucky to find the most brilliant local joiner who completely understood my ideas and had fantastic ideas of his own.' Peter Bennett has built an acreage of cupboards that are so discreetly minimalist you barely notice their existence. A whole room downstairs has been lined with them and guests sent to find something have been known to return asking where the cupboards are. These particular cupboards hide the freezer, overflow from the kitchen 'and everything, from Tupperware boxes to plasters, that I don't want to see', says Maddie.

A tour of the house reveals the same design of cupboard filling alcoves, lining walls and marching along both sides of the landing. Elsewhere, Peter Bennett has made a sleek wall unit that hides the wires and boxes beneath the wall-mounted television,

THIS PAGE and OPPOSITE The farmhouse is built on sloping land and rooms downstairs are on different levels. The kitchen is on the highest level and stone stairs lead up from it to a long landing linking the first floor bedrooms and bathroom. Behind the staircase, steps lead down to the 'room of cupboards', a second bathroom and the all-important boot and coat room next to the back door. Further steps lead down into the living room and dining room. The openings without doors between rooms give the house an almost open-plan feel. The garden can be glimpsed through the front door at the end of the cross passage just beyond the dining table.

OPPOSITE A spare bedroom spans the house, its ceiling opened up into the roof. Rugs from IKEA are laid over the carpet, and one of the vintage patchwork quilts that Maddie collects covers a sofa from Heal's on the right. The matching wardrobes and bedroom cabinet are vintage Heal's, bought by Maddie from an advertisement in the local paper. There is a view from this bedroom all the way down to Iris's bedroom at the other end of the house.

ABOVE In the same bedroom, a delicate mobile by Dan Chadwick, a present to David and Maddie from the artist, is suspended from the ancient roof beams.

ABOVE RIGHT The low window in the bathroom affords bathers a view over the garden from the tub.

a shelving unit designed to corral shoes and boots, and racks to hold the great stacks of logs that are devoured by the wood-burning stoves in the living room and playroom.

Maddie's style is clean and streamlined, but she is also immensely practical and loves the organic feel of the house, parts of which probably date back a good 400 years. The furnishings are entirely in keeping with this aesthetic, a mix of warm vintage pieces, including Ercol, and rugs and cushions from IKEA. 'I hate having to worry if a child spills something – I wanted an interior that was really comfortable, but also bomb-proof.'

The clever mix of old and new – a delicate Dan Chadwick mobile hanging amidst rustic, wrinkled beams, a low Heal's sofa echoed by a quaintly oblong alcove in a wavering plaster wall, a sleek bent plywood chair beside a battered oak door – is engaging and very chic. And it's all the more impressive when you learn that most of the furnishings were bought inexpensively from advertisements spotted in the local paper.

Slowly they are restoring the outbuildings. The threshing barn is home to the trampoline, where you can bounce away with one of the loveliest views you could wish for. The vegetable garden has been cleared, rabbit-proofed and cultivated, and Devon Red cattle from the neighbouring farm graze their fields. Last year they nursed three orphan lambs until they were big enough to go back to the farm. Both David and Maddie still regularly return to London for work, but it is quite obvious that their hearts are here, among the sheep and the buttercups.

COUNTRY CONTRAST

ABOVE and FAR RIGHT The previous occupant of the farmhouse was an artist and a great lover of trees, and planted many different varieties of tree on the land around the house. Alison has inherited a love of gardening from her father and has created a vegetable garden in the old walled garden next to the stables.

OPPOSITE The pantry next to the kitchen is invaluable storage space and where Alison keeps kitchen gadgets such as the coffee maker. Ugly modern packaging, however, is banished inside metal boxes, leaving the original wooden shelving free of anything that does not fit the strict aesthetic of a house where everything seems to have been arranged in a pleasing still life. Walls are painted in Farrow & Ball's Mouse's Back, and the yellow bowls and tin take on extra vibrancy in a colour scheme that is otherwise muted.

Alison Hill seems an unlikely devotee of rural living. Her house in London is sleek and minimalist, and her job as Head of Home Design for Debenhams requires a beagle's nose for sniffing out future trends. Surely she needs to be permanently plugged into the design zeitgeist, and where better to find it than London? 'Not necessarily,' she says. 'In 2010, I was looking at the statistics for the number of people going to music festivals and farm shops, and this inspired a collection we referred to as "field to fork". I study everything from leisure activities to what is on the menu at local pubs, just to get a feel for what is going on in people's heads. And I am lucky enough to be able to live in the town and the country, so I can be in touch with both.'

Alison and her husband John, a company secretary, have been renting a diminutive and thoroughly rustic farm on the edge of marshland in Suffolk for the last two years and spend as much time there as they can with no other house, let alone shopping opportunity, in sight. 'I was brought up in Beckenham, although we used to spend our holidays on my father's family's farm on Jersey, and Suffolk is a part of the country I didn't know at all. I discovered this area when I worked for Dunhill, because one of the two factories that supplied silk for Dunhill ties was based in Sudbury – the other was in Como in Italy. We started coming down here for weekends and began a real love affair with the place. Then we thought we should try renting somewhere and we looked for a long time but didn't see anything that really appealed. Our main criteria was that it had to be isolated, so when we met the estate agent for this house at the end of the track that leads to it, I already knew I wanted it.'

The track leads off a lane and through the flat, low-lying fields that once belonged to the farm and on which the farmer grazed his suckler herds. At the very end of the track, the warm pink, corrugated pantiles of the farm roof stand out against a backdrop of tall, feathery willow trees, silver birch, sweet chestnut and acer. Alison has worked hard on the

ABOVE LEFT The house is timber-framed and many of the walls as well as the ceilings have exposed beams.

ABOVE RIGHT A pair of Habitat sofas face one another on either side of the living room inglenook. A few carefully chosen antique pieces, such as the three-legged stool next to the fireplace, add another dimension to the furnishings.

BELOW LEFT Alison has planted a deep raised border at the edge of the brick terrace in front of the house.

OPPOSITE The kitchen retains its Victorian bread oven and an old butler's sink, but an Aga has replaced the original cooking range. The chairs are from Designers Guild.

garden, cultivating a deep raised border edging the brick terrace at the front, while allowing the grass at the back to melt into the trees and undergrowth, which form an amphitheatre of green. Brick and flint farm buildings cluster to one side, the largest now used as a wood store and propagating shed, while the old stables shelter one edge of the walled vegetable garden that Alison has tended from wilderness.

The house is plain on the outside, cream with black-painted, small-paned casement windows. Inside, its age is more apparent. The porch opens straight into the living room, with its wide brick inglenook. On the other side of the entrance is the kitchen, which has a brick floor and a heavily beamed ceiling. A downstairs bedroom has a wall of exposed brick and timber, and the scullery beyond the kitchen still retains its weathered wooden shelving, its walls and low ceiling crisscrossed by a framework of slim wooden beams and uprights. There are two tiny, steep wooden staircases, a legacy of when the building was divided into separate cottages, and upstairs the ceilings are even lower, with doors between rooms that even a ten-year-old might need to duck to get through.

ABOVE At an early stage in its history, the farmhouse was divided into two cottages and has two narrow and very steep staircases. In order to get beds and larger pieces of furniture upstairs, the lower steps had to be temporarily dismantled and replaced. This staircase leads up from the living room. The porch is through the door to the left, the kitchen through the door to the right. The flower painting next to the door to the kitchen is by Norma Jameson and the landscape painting above the sofa is by Richard Tuff.

OPPOSITE ABOVE LEFT A rug and a cube stool echo the red of a Craigie Aitchison print in an upstairs study area.

OPPOSITE ABOVE RIGHT At the top of the stairs from the living room, the rooms lead one into the other.

OPPOSITE BELOW Drawings by Alison of her cats are propped on an old trestle table on an upstairs landing.

Into these small, cottagey spaces, with their primitive, rough plaster and pitted woodwork, Alison has placed a spare and sophisticated selection of furnishings, ceramics, textiles and contemporary art; white and dark grey plastic chairs from Designers Guild in the kitchen; a pair of straight-edged Habitat sofas in the sitting room; sleek little ceramic bowls in bright jewel colours on a beam in a bathroom; another group of contemporary ceramics in primrose yellow and lime green on a bedroom mantelpiece; a glass-topped desk and leather swivel chair in an upstairs study. Beds are made up with smart linen and modern quilts. In the larder, shiny metal boxes, perfectly lined up on the quarry-tiled floor, hide the mess of modern food packaging, while rice, pasta, muesli and couscous have been decanted into neat rows of preserving jars.

The contrast between the shiny and the rough-hewn, the straight-lined and the wobbly-edged, the uneven and the perfectly smooth, the very old and the brand new, is a recurring theme. Colours are equally carefully juxtaposed, whether the vibrant yellow of a tin and matching bowls that jumps out from the neutral shades and natural materials of the scullery,

THIS PAGE All the upstairs bedrooms have low ceilings incorporating the slope of the roof, and all have double beds piled with pillows and made up with stylish bedlinen and quilts from the Debenhams home design range, of which Alison is the head. Again, the contrast between the fresh, luxurious modernity of the well-dressed beds and the rough plaster, beams and cottage proportions of the rooms is what gives these spaces their particular charm and character.

a moss green velvet bedspread that echoes the colours in a painted seascape on the wall above or the red of a Craigie Aitchison print repeated in the red leather upholstery of a cube-shaped stool. Alison's unerring eye for balance and composition, for making patterns with her placing of objects and combining of colours, is apparent in every room, and even though all they have done is to furnish the house and paint the walls in a palette of Farrow & Ball off-whites, she and John have made the place very much their own.

Nonetheless, they won't be staying. They have at last found a house they want to buy, not far away. 'I think I have a genetic connection with the countryside,' Alison states. 'My father was brought up on a farm and his brother and sister are both farmers. My sister and I both had Jersey cows named after us. Mine was the cow that was used on the Jersey [postage] stamp.'

ABOVE The moss green velvet quilt in this downstairs spare bedroom picks up the colours of the seascape above the bed. The print of cats is by Elizabeth Blackadder, one of several images of cats in the house. One of Alison and John's criteria when looking for a house to rent was somewhere they felt their own cats, a tortoiseshell called Lily and an Egyptian cat called Yasmin, could settle.

RIGHT The door into this upstairs bathroom is so low that even a child has to stoop to step through it.

NO FRILLS FARMHOUSE
elements of style

- **STORAGE** Places to hide the unsightly clutter the rest of us leave lying around are essential to the clean lines of this disciplined look. Maddie and David have commissioned bespoke storage from cabinet maker Peter Bennett, including a sleek wall cupboard beneath the television to hide wires and DVDs, a headboard for their bed incorporating hidden shelves and a 'room of cupboards' just outside their kitchen. Alison Hill stores groceries in a row of large metal boxes in her pantry. Eva Johnson and Bella Pringle appear to be naturally tidy and also the kind of women who own wardrobes of beautifully edited clothing rather than keeping everything in case it comes back into fashion/fits again at some unknown future date.

- **FLOORING** Plain floors in wood or stone, softened with the occasional, strategically placed rug, give an interior a simple, unadorned feel. Eva Johnson has used Swedish lye to bleach and seal the original floorboards throughout her house. Bella Pringle, however, only has original floorboards upstairs. Downstairs, the floors are sheets of chipboard, which she has painted with durable floor paint, an option that also works well for disguising floorboards that are patched and mismatched.

- **SIMPLE STATEMENTS** In an otherwise plain room, anything decorative has extra impact. In Bella Pringle's bedroom, it is the cut-out silhouette of a Suffolk Punch horse that pulls the eye and is all the more striking for the lack of other visual distractions. Alison Hill creates a similar focal point with a trio of brightly coloured ceramic bowls on a beam in her bathroom.

- **COLOURS** Eva Johnson's house achieves its visual serenity partly as a result of a strict colour scheme of shades of off-white, grey and brown, with only occasional highlights of blue or tiny touches of other colours, such as red in the stripe of a cushion. Bella Pringle's colour schemes are equally restrained, particularly in the kitchen, where she uses subtle shades of off-white paint to unite a disparate selection of antique cupboards, tables, cabinets and shelves.

- **CURTAINS** Shutters, blinds or simple, unlined curtains are the least fussy window treatments. Eva Johnson takes the minimal curtain to extremes in her bathroom where a tea towel is pegged to a window bar, while the fine white cotton curtains in her bedroom are not only semi-transparent, they are too narrow to pull right across the windows. This is not an option for anyone whose sleep is disturbed by daylight, but the effect is delightfully impromptu.

- **TO PAINT OR NOT TO PAINT** Wooden beams can either be painted the same colour as walls, as in Bella Pringle's bedroom and Eva Johnson's dining room, or left as bare wood, in which case if they are old they will be dark and provide strong contrast with a pale wall colour. The two effects are very different: one emphasizes the architecture and structure of a room, while the other minimizes it. Dark, heavy ceiling beams can have a slightly claustrophobic effect if the ceiling is already on the low side.

FUNKY
FARMHOUSE

THE OLD ENGLISH FARMHOUSE, WITH ITS BEAMS, ITS STONE FLOORS, ITS INGLENOOK FIREPLACES AND PRACTICAL, NO-NONSENSE ARCHITECTURE, IS ABOUT AS ICONIC AS IT GETS WHEN IT COMES TO CLASSIC COUNTRY STYLE. SOME OWNERS TAKE THIS AS THEIR CUE TO STAY SAFE AND TRADITIONAL WITH THEIR INTERIOR DESIGN; OTHERS GO OFF IN ANOTHER DIRECTION ALTOGETHER. THE FOLLOWING FARMHOUSES HAVE NO LACK OF BEAMS, INGLENOOKS AND FLAGSTONES, BUT THEIR OWNERS HAVE DECORATED THEM IN THEIR OWN DISTINCTIVE TASTES, UNDAUNTED BY THE WEIGHT OF HISTORY OR EXPECTATION, WITH RESULTS THAT ARE BOTH EXCITING AND SURPRISING.

BARNYARD BAROQUE

ABOVE Looking past a Mark Brazier-Jones console table and candelabra on the upstairs corridor towards a spare bedroom painted gloss red.

ABOVE RIGHT The panelling and 'parquet' floor in Julia's study were made from old builders' pallets.

OPPOSITE The kitchen typifies the slightly alarming mix of rustic charm and all-out glamour that characterizes the house, with its giant chandelier hanging low over a pine table in front of the roughly plastered chimney breast and dark green Aga. Equally typical are the visual jokes: a glittery tiara crowning the toothy leer of the stuffed boar's head, and a prim Victorian needlework fire-screen, embroidered with the words 'Thou shalt not kill' hanging from the same hook as a rifle.

The estate agent's brochure for the farmhouse Mark Brazier-Jones and Julia Lowery bought two years ago shows an unremarkable if attractive house, long and low, painted palest pastel pink, surrounded by clipped hedges and tidy topiary. The pastel pink has survived, but in other respects the place is barely recognizable. The topiary has gone — 'we trashed the garden', says Julia. In its place are three caravans, one a silver Airstream, various cars including a vintage Ford pick-up and chickens pecking peaceably in the long grass. The interior of the house has undergone an even more violent transformation; from bland teacher's pet to raunchy, Gothic rebel — rarely can the personality of a house have changed so drastically in so short a time.

Well known in the design world for his glamorous, baroque metal furniture and lighting, Mark Brazier-Jones claims that the first thing he did after moving into his South Cambridgeshire farmhouse was to take a hatchet to the hall. 'The interior was very peach, very '70s, all flat walls and lino floors,' he explains. 'It needed to be roughed up a bit, so I started knocking corners off.

ABOVE Mark designed and built the staircase that rises from the middle of the living room just in time for a photo shoot, using rugged timber treads supported by delicate ironwork. The entrance hall, which they painted bright turquoise after Mark had 'distressed' it with a hatchet, can just be seen to the left of the chimney breast.

RIGHT The panelling and the floor in the living room were installed by Mark and Julia, and are not as old as they look. The sofa with its integral lamp, the coffee table, the table lamp and the pink chaise longue in the background are all designs by Mark. Smoke from the banqueting hall beyond the kitchen can be seen billowing through the door.

The farmer who owned it had done it up for his daughter,' he continues. 'He had done all the hard work, including digging down in the living room to get more ceiling height, but there was no patina.'

Thanks to the hatchet, plus many rather more subtle modifications, the interior now has patina on a grand scale, and executed with such convincing panache it is a genuine shock to discover how much of it is a recent creation. In the kitchen, for example, where the ceiling rises into the slope of the roof, there is a roughly plastered arched chimneypiece with a giant, gnarled beam of a mantelshelf that you feel sure must be Tudor, if not medieval. A glance back at the brochure, however, shows that until Mark got his hands on it, the fireplace was a slightly prissy brick affair. What appears to be old panelling in the living room was made by sticking pieces of wood from builders' pallets straight onto the wallpaper. The original oak floorboards are in fact new oak floorboards, professionally 'tumbled' to knock them about a bit, their tongue-and-groove edges sawn off, stained dark brown, stuck down with glue and adorned with some strategically placed nails. More thick plaster with the texture of hastily spread clotted cream adds faux historical texture to the inglenook in the living room.

So much for the rough, but what makes these interiors so intriguing is the way it contrasts with the smooth, as the rustic architecture of the rooms repeatedly clashes with the gloss and sophistication of their contents. In the living room, facing the inglenook, crouches a massive L-shaped sofa, upholstered in a moss green velvet stripe, its frame made from curling, gilded metal, an integral chandelier of crystal balls suspended from a metal arm that swoops up and over from its corner. Embroidered cushions are heaped along one side and a coffee table with a top of thick, bevelled glass rests on elegantly

THIS PICTURE Despite the cottage proportions of the main bedroom, with its low and sloping ceiling, its small window and beamed wall, Mark and Julia have gone for Hollywood glamour. The polished aluminium bed with its dragons, pineapples, curlicues and crystal balls is one of Mark's creations, and he also made the legs for the shop-bought mirrored furnishings. Walls are mirrored on one side of the room, facing mirrored wardrobes on the wall opposite, and by the light of a crystal chandelier the whole rooms sparkles.

OPPOSITE LEFT and RIGHT The barn attached to the kitchen end of the house was being used to store tractors, but Mark and Julia have annexed it to create an extra room for entertaining on a grand scale. The walls are painted a moody dark aubergine and the enormously long dining table is surrounded by an assortment of splendid chairs, some designed by Mark, others antique. Lit by candles, the effect is Gormenghast in a barn.

BELOW Another Pegasus chair and an intricate wall clock, also by Mark, adorn the end of the upstairs corridor with a view into the bathroom beyond.

BOTTOM There are more reflective surfaces in the bathroom, which is lined with glassy dark green tiles, cut perfectly to follow the wavering edges of the ancient beams, making a striking contrast between their strict geometry and the organic architecture.

muscular, metal legs with hoofed feet. At the other end of the room, beyond the curve of the spiral staircase, reclines a lounge-lizard of a chaise longue, tasselled, gilded and upholstered in buttoned, fuchsia pink pony-skin. A glittering, bowl-shaped chandelier the size of a tractor wheel hangs low over the kitchen table in front of the faux medieval chimneypiece. The stairs themselves twist upwards, their treads rugged slices of tree trunk supported by delicate metalwork with pineapple finials and a gracefully twirling banister rail – again, that combination of the rough with the smooth.

Upstairs, the game of compare and contrast continues with a mirrored boudoir, glitzy enough for an old-fashioned Hollywood starlet, inserted into a room with beamed walls, a low cottage window and a sloping ceiling. Next door is a Chinese-themed bedroom, painted gloss red and with a headboard upholstered in turquoise velvet embossed with raised circles of Chinese silk embroidery. The third bedroom is a little more restrained, black with an ornate metal bed, decorated with framed glamour girls from 1940s calendars. These rooms are linked by a corridor, with the same sloping ceiling and low windows. Against the dark grey of the walls, three more pieces of highly wrought metal furniture catch the light, glinting and glossy like celebrities at a small country wedding; one a wall clock, one a console with legs forked and shiny as bolts of lightning, one a chair with a back in the shape of a pair of wings. Like all the metal furniture, wall lights and chandeliers, they are Mark's designs, and look peculiarly at home, if not entirely appropriate, in this modest, rustic house in the midst of the English countryside.

The house has one further surprise. Through a door next to the kitchen fireplace is a vast, dark dining room converted from an adjoining barn. Banqueting hall would be a better description. 'The previous owners kept a couple of tractors in here,' says Julia, 'but we could see its potential.' Mark built a baronial fireplace, which smokes in an appropriately medieval manner, and they painted the walls and ceiling in a single weekend, teetering on ladders and using a spray gun, which has left tiny freckles on the crystal balls of the low-hanging chandeliers. Here, at a long table lit by candelabra, seated on a variety of throne-like chairs, guests gather for evening feasts that may entail dancing on the table and competitions to see who can shoot out a candle flame with an air gun from the other end of the house. There is no swinging from the chandeliers, but Julia says that two particularly acrobatic guests did once manage to navigate the ceiling beams from one end of the room to the other before settling astride the stuffed moose's head over the fireplace.

OPPOSITE The ground floor consists of three large rooms leading one into the other, and a back entrance porch with a downstairs cloakroom, which was added by the previous owner, Joe Orsi, who stayed on to build it after Paul Vogel and Sam Denny-Hodson moved in. Joe also rebuilt the Tudor brick fireplace in this living room at one end of the house. Looking past the oak spiral staircase, there is a view into the central 'snug', where Sam has her office. The campaign chair was bought in Camden, London.

RIGHT The dining end of the kitchen is in a lean-to extension.

ABOVE The eldest of their three sons, Felix, has a bedroom under the steeply sloping beams of the end gable.

BELOW Seen from outside, the gable that encloses Felix's bedroom is as steep and pointed as a witch's hat. The house is timber-framed and Tudor, and was stripped back to its frame and expertly restored by its former owner. In front of the house, lawn slopes down to a paddock and a quiet country road. Behind the house are barns and outbuildings that have been converted into stylish holiday cottages and a studio for Paul.

MODERN MATTERS

Sam Denny-Hodson is not one to dither or to do things by half measures. Ten years ago, as a diehard city girl with a glamorous job in fashion PR, a collection of high heels and handbags straight from the pages of Vogue and a diary packed with parties, she took a weekend break in Suffolk and found herself sitting on the beach with her first baby and deciding they should move to the country. Meanwhile, her music-mad husband Paul Vogel was camped out at the Glastonbury Festival, where he got a call the next day to say she had bought a cottage by the sea. What he did not yet know was that not only had Sam bought a cottage, she was already making plans for them to leave London altogether.

Their country relocation house-hunt started in earnest during the summer of 2003, and by February 2004 Sam and Paul had moved. 'We had a four-year-old, an eight-month-old baby and just after we came here I discovered I was pregnant with our third son, which wasn't ideal,' Sam comments wryly, 'but fortunately, the house was in excellent structural shape.' This was entirely thanks to its previous owner Joe Orsi, a historic buildings enthusiast, who over the course of some years had literally taken the house apart and put it back together again, and in the process turned himself into a skilled blacksmith, builder and expert in the conservation and restoration of early, timber-framed buildings.

LEFT The central 'snug' is defined by the strong verticals of the wooden mullioned windows and the horizontals of the ceiling beams, all of which slope in slightly different directions. Sam's office, from where she works as a casting director and runs a holiday letting business, is opposite the fireplace, the books on the shelves above artfully colour-coded.

RIGHT The room is furnished with vintage finds including two leather sofas, one from Collingwood Cotehele, the other from Diss auction house, and an Eames lounger, which was bought in America and shipped over, a more affordable option than buying one here. The Paul Smith for The Rug Company needlework cushion with birds was an eBay purchase, and the folded rug is a design by Paul Vogel who specializes in checks and stripes for fashion and furnishings. The door to the right of the fireplace leads into a small front hall with a front door that is rarely used.

Sam and Paul made an instant decision that they wanted to buy the house on the day that they viewed it. Joe was a slightly reluctant seller, but he agreed to let them have it on the condition that they allowed him to stay on to build the porch he had been planning to add at the back. He moved into an outbuilding he had converted into a cottage, and lived there for six months as resident builder, friend and general country guru, advising them on everything from where to shop to how they should be sure not to paint the natural oak window frames.

As recently as the 1980s, the house was a working farm. The farmer who was born there still lives locally and has kept most of the land, which is now 'set-aside' and neither cultivated nor grazed, only cut once a year. Generously, he allows it to be used for activities from kite flying to space for the local model aeroplane society. 'It's like being surrounded by our own parkland,' says Paul. 'It's great for the boys, and for walking the dogs.'

The farmhouse is a striking building, standing in open fields, slightly elevated above the country road that runs in front of it, with a three-storey gable as steep as a witch's hat at one end and a lower, long façade leading off to the left pierced with windows of different shapes and sizes and at slightly different heights. Another interested buyer had wanted to use the house as the setting for a horror film, and there is something slightly spooky about its crooked, ancient exterior, like an Arthur Rackham illustration of a house inhabited by a mysterious sorcerer.

Any sense that you might be entering some museum-piece reconstruction is instantly dispelled the moment you step from the smart, new porch into the living room, which is the oldest part of the house, dating from the 1400s. Architecturally, the interior is as quaint as the exterior, with timber framing and beams, an arched brick fireplace and wooden mullioned windows. The contents of the room, however, are colourful and contemporary: two vintage leather sofas piled with cushions, an Eames lounger and stool, a wall of metal shelving incorporating a computer desk and on the walls modern prints and black and white photographs of The Rolling Stones in various states of drug-enhanced relaxation lolling around a French chateau.

Next to this, just beyond the wooden spiral staircase, is a living room with another big brick fireplace. Here there is an L-shaped Terence Woodgate sofa decked with cushions in bold, African batik, and on the walls more black and white photographs on a rock and roll theme, including images of David Bowie and Led Zeppelin, and a row of silk-screen portraits of the Beatles in neon colours.

On the other side of the central 'snug' is the kitchen, which they were given permission to extend with a further timber bay and have stretched even further with a single-storey, lean-to extension. Sitting at the rustic kitchen table, on a slick chrome and leather chair, Sam says that this room, with its painted wood cupboards and dresser, is as 'country' as she can be comfortable with. 'I went bonkers when we first moved

OPPOSITE When Sam and Paul first bought the house, the kitchen was the smallest of the three downstairs rooms. Fortunately, they gained permission to extend the room by one further timber bay, marked by the distance between the ceiling beams running laterally across the space, as when it was first built in the 16th century the house would have included this extra bay. The wall hung with maps is the original outer wall, to which they were allowed to add a lean-to extension giving space for a long dining table. Sam and Paul have nothing but praise for builders Blyth Valley Renovations. 'They were

amazing at answering my many "how do we put a shower/dressing room/floor into a ridiculously wonky space",' she says.

ABOVE RIGHT Sam describes the bathroom as her 'retreat', although she is often joined there by at least one of their four dogs. The floor still has a large trapdoor through which, they have been told, animals were once hoisted to be wintered on an upper floor. Thanks to Scott Baxter Plumbing and Heating, Sam says they have managed to install underfloor heating, showers and bathrooms where no one else thought it possible.

and decorated in a sort of opium den version of traditional, with orange velvet sofas and over-the-top curtains, but a couple of years ago I woke up one morning in New York and realized it just wasn't me.'

The moment she got back she took down the curtains and raided the barn from where Paul runs his business as a textile designer for the furniture they had brought with them from their Clerkenwell loft. Now Paul can seat visiting customers, who range from Top Shop and Jack Wills to Ralph Lauren and Missoni, on orange velvet sofas at one end of his huge studio. And the house is a vibrant, glossy mongrel, half city slicker, half country cousin, which is just how they like it.

THIS PICTURE The main bedroom is above the living room at one end of the house and the floor slopes particularly violently, rising like the swell of the ocean in the middle and falling away at the edges. The bed sits beneath one of three windows and there is a view from it of distant fields and trees rising up to the horizon. The crystal wall lights, which Sam has used throughout the house, were from Graham & Green. The photograph on the left of the bed is of Picasso on the beach, and the butterfly picture next to the door is by Lisa J. Barnes.

CHIC & CHEERFUL

ABOVE LEFT Next to the more formal living room downstairs is a 'snug' that is almost filled by a deep corner sofa piled with cushions and, in front of it, a buttoned velvet footstool from George Smith. Facing the sofa is a wall-mounted flat-screen television.

ABOVE RIGHT Just outside the front door, Joanna found a stone-lined well, which she uncovered and built a low wall around.

FAR RIGHT The house has cottage proportions and retains its original planked doors, here seen open onto an upstairs corridor. The shiny metal door handles are Joanna's addition.

OPPOSITE In the roof space, lit by dormer windows, Joanna has created a suite of bathroom and bedroom with, between them, this sitting room, which is furnished with a characteristically interesting mix of pieces, including a pair of Victorian buttoned armchairs from Amy Perry Antiques. The glass dome encloses gold foil flowers and part of a broken china doll. A step leads up into the bathroom, with its antique copper bathtub.

Behind the Aga in the kitchen of Joanna Berryman's Cotswold farmhouse is a big sheet of mirror glass. This impertinent juxtaposition of country kitchen deity and city bling could be vulgar but isn't. In fact, the effect is handsome, a refreshing change from the more usual blue and white wobbly tiles decorated with hand-painted rabbits, and a testament to interior designer Joanna's eye for a bold, decorative gesture. Adding to the sheen of this large, light room are work surfaces in smooth white marble and splashbacks of shiny, white brick-shaped tiles. Undercutting the gloss is a well-used butcher's block that functions as a kitchen island, its top so worn by years of cutting and chopping that anything placed on it is likely to slide off again.

Joanna fondly describes the house as 'a bit of a Frankenstein', by which she means it has been added to over the centuries to become an architectural hybrid. Unlike the monster, however, this mix-and-match creature is delightfully pretty, built in golden stone with a façade that may date back as far as the 17th century under a roof of stone tiles cushioned with moss and speckled with lichen. There is a stone barn facing the house, which Joanna has converted into an office and extra guest accommodation, and there is an ancient well to the right of the front door.

'I have always liked this part of the country,' Joanna says. 'And I was looking for a bolt-hole to escape to from London at weekends. This was the last of several properties I viewed and the one I fell in love with. I saw it on one of those beautiful autumnal days when everything seems gilded, and I knew I wanted to buy it before I even stepped inside. I loved the location – down its own little road, but on the edge of a pretty village – I loved the tennis court, and I loved the fact that the house has cottage proportions but also a feeling of light and space. We exchanged contracts over New Year 2010, and the builders started work the next day.'

Joanna made very few structural changes. Rather than major cosmetic surgery, what the house required was a gentle face-lift and some glamorous make-up. Out went all the fitted carpets to be replaced by stone and reclaimed floorboards downstairs, and sisal matting upstairs. In went bookcases, a raised slate hearth in the inglenook and antique bathroom fittings. With walls painted in Farrow & Ball's Hardwick White and French Gray, the scene was set for the furnishings, many of which were bought locally.

Joanna's is not a conventional take on country house style. She has used some of its elements – there are paintings and sculptures of horses, antlers, big

RIGHT In the living room, Joanna has solved the common problem of a smoking inglenook by raising the hearth on slabs of slate resting on dry stone supports. The room is cosy and tactile, with fabrics in contrasting textures: rough sackcloth on the squashy window seat cushion, cotton velvet on the deeply padded stool, silk ikat on the chairs and a soft rabbit fur throw draped over the back of the sofa. The huge book resting on the stool is Vivienne Westwood's *Opus*.

cushioned sofas, an old pine dresser in the kitchen, a brass bed in one of the bedrooms – but the effect is far from traditional. The equine theme, for example, is announced in the living room by a vibrant 1950s oil painting of two white horses against a scarlet background. Two large, sculpted horse's heads, one terracotta, one bronze, arch their necks on top of a small desk in the same room, while a pair of crystal horses rear up on a side table. Over the door is a ceramic tile with a lustre silhouette of a horse, and there is also a metal relief plaque of a racehorse hung above a plant stand supporting a vintage typewriter. One of the bedrooms has a metal bed moulded to look like harness facing a giant oil painting of a hunting scene. As for the antlers, the skulls to which they are attached are studded with crystals, while the pine dresser is stacked with cookery books and contemporary white crockery from Made, and is watched over by a rather kitsch painting of The Madonna.

LEFT The hall at the back of the house opens into a large utility room to the right. The door ahead is open into the kitchen where the wall to the left has been painted with blackboard paint and acts as a giant memo board.

ABOVE The kitchen is an L-shaped room at the back of the house, the portion beyond the old ceiling beam a glass-roofed extension that allows light to flood into the space from above. Behind the Aga Joanna has installed a

wall of mirror glass, which reflects more light and visually extends the space, making the room seem twice as long. Orange Le Creuset pots, pans, casseroles and kettle almost glow against a background of glossy white. The butcher's block shows its age with a surface worn away by years of use.

OPPOSITE Off the kitchen is a dining area with French doors that lead out onto a terrace where there is another table for alfresco summer dining.

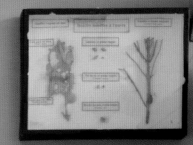
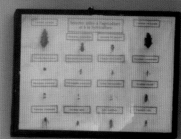

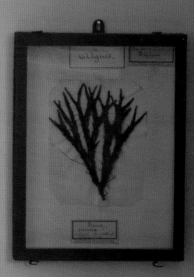

On the top floor, under the steep sloping beams of the roof, the glamour quotient reaches its apogee. Here Joanna has created a suite of bedroom, bathroom and sitting room, the mood of which she describes as '*Boogie Nights* meets Marie Antoinette' with a gilded bed from Graham & Green, an antique copper bathtub and her signature mix of antiques, unusual vintage pieces and visual jokes, like the grey knitted lampshade and the cushions printed with Edwardian portraits.

As glamorous as her rooms, and the ex-wife of Coldplay's bassist Guy Berryman, Joanna is still a relative newcomer in the world of interior design, having started her career in fashion. But her young, modish yet comfortable style is already in demand and her company, Matrushka, is juggling half a dozen or more projects that, at the time of writing, include a Gothic lodge in Barnes for a sports celebrity, a house in Maida Vale and a shop for trendy tailor Gresham Blake on Commercial Street in London.

Initially designed as a country retreat for Joanna, her daughter Nico, her family and friends, the moment pictures of The Folly appeared in a magazine people were clamouring to rent it. Joanna has since found that she is happy to share it, as she says guests are so appreciative, and she is pleased that it has become a successful commercial venture, albeit almost by accident. 'I had been planning to spend Christmas there this year,' she says almost plaintively from her studio in London, 'but I have had an offer I can't refuse, so I will probably go to Sri Lanka instead!'

ABOVE Another unusual antique bathtub in polished copper, bought at Ardingly antiques fair, tucks under the sloping roof of the attic bathroom.

LEFT The equine theme that recurs throughout the house is represented in this bedroom by the 'Handel' bed from And So To Bed, which is made to resemble harness. The painting hanging opposite the foot of the bed is a hunting scene, and the luscious pink velvet bedspread is Matthew Williamson for Debenhams.

OPPOSITE All the bathrooms feature charming antique fittings, such as this roll-top bathtub with its giant, fixed shower head from Catchpole & Rye. Joanna has lined the room with painted matchboarding, on which she has hung framed Edwardian prints, and emphasized the old-fashioned, feminine feel of the room with a broderie anglaise shower curtain.

FUNKY FARMHOUSE
elements of style

• SURPRISE A surprise may be good or bad, but is invariably intriguing. Behind their demure, period exteriors, all of these houses hide unexpected interiors, whether Clerkenwell-loft contemporary, louche neo-baroque or rock-chick chic. Making this culture clash a good surprise is a matter of having the courage of your convictions allied with the visual sensitivity to ensure that the architecture and period character of an interior are enhanced and highlighted by the contrast, rather than swamped and dominated.

• CONTRAST While the headline contrast in these interiors is between their architecture and the style in which they have been furnished and decorated, each also features contrast at a more detailed level, whether the polished contemporary door handles on Joanna Berryman's cottage-style doors, or the glitzy Venetian mirror propped in the rustic fireplace of Sam Denny Hodson and Paul Vogel's bedroom. Often the contrast is between textures as well as styles, and this is a particular feature of Mark Brazier-Jones and Julia Lowery's farmhouse, where rough, rustic plaster and timber are the setting for high-gloss furnishings.

• WIT When a witty gesture falls flat, it sinks into pretension. Battered straw hats balanced on the heads of marble busts are more likely to prompt a groan than an appreciative chuckle. The diamond tiara on Mark Brazier-Jones' stuffed boar's head, however, is definitely worth a smile, as is the sheer incongruity of photographs of rock legends Keith Richards and Charlie Watts staring from the Tudor brickwork of a wooden staircase in Sam Denny Hodson and Paul Vogel's Suffolk farmhouse. Joanna Berryman spices the shopping lists scribbled on the blackboard paint that covers a wall of her kitchen with joky comments such as 'Charles and Camilla for tea!'; a reference to the proximity of Highgrove.

• ODDITIES Both Mark Brazier-Jones and Joanna Berryman have elevated early 20th-century typewriters to the status of ornament by placing them on pedestals (plant stands). They both also like to put strange things inside Victorian glass domes, in Joanna Berryman's case bits of broken doll, in Mark Brazier-Jones' a bird's skull and the wire from a champagne cork among other things. Changing the context of an object invites you to look at it afresh – whether a urinal in an art gallery, or a typewriter on a pedestal.

• SCALE According to Mark Brazier-Jones a chandelier can never be too big. 'The mistake most people make with chandeliers is too small, hung too high,' he says. Neither are mistakes he could be accused of in his own house. The chandelier in his kitchen, for example, is the size of a tractor wheel and hangs over the table at the level of the mantelpiece. None of these owners are afraid of scale. Sam Denny Hodson and Paul Vogel hang pictures that nearly fill their allocated bits of wall, while Joanna Berryman fits huge sofas and giant beds into small rooms.

DIRECTORY OF UK & US SOURCES

Many of the house owners featured in this book are skilled at DIY, and also adept at recycling things, adapting things, and finding bargains at boot fairs and charity shops. They all also cite local antique shops, antiques centres, and auction houses as the source of many of their furnishings. These would be far too numerous to mention individually, and you doubtless have your own favourites.

ARCHITECTURAL SALVAGE

Architectural Accents
2711 Piedmont Road NE
Atlanta, GA 30305
(+1) 404 266 8700
www.architectural accents.com

Antique light fixtures, door hardware, garden antiques and other reclaimed items.

Castle Reclamation
Parrett Works
Martock
Somerset TA12 6AE
+44 (0)1935 826483
www.castlereclamation.com

Reclaimed items and materials, including oak and flagstones for flooring, fireplace surrounds and unusual finds such as tapestries and statuary.

LASSCO
Brunswick House
30 Wandsworth Road
London SW8 2LG
+44 (0)20 7394 2100
www.lassco.co.uk

One of the first and still one of the best; everything from fireplaces to floors to stained glass and panelling.

Original Architectural Antiques Company
Ermin Farm
Cirencester
Gloucestershire GL7 5PN
+44 (0)1285 869222
www.originaluk.com

Reclaimed oak beams, fireplaces and limestone troughs.

Architectural Salvage Company
1840 W Hubbard St
Chicago, IL 60622
(+1) 312 733 0098
www.salvageone.com

Salvaged architectural elements, vintage furniture and fittings.

BATHROOMS

Antique Baths of Ivybridge
Erme Bridge Works
Ermington Road
Ivybridge
Devon PL21 9DE
+44 (0)1752 698250
www.antiquebaths.com

Reconditioned antique baths and sanitary ware plus reproduction ranges.

Balineum
+44 (0)20 74319364
www.balineum.co.uk

Online bathroom fittings and accessories, and a range of pretty hand-painted tiles.

Catchpole & Rye
Saracens Dairy
Jobbs Lane
Pluckley
Kent TN27 0SA
+44 (0)1233 840444
www.crye.co.uk

Antique and reproduction sanitary ware, including antique cast-iron baths and metal baths poured in the on-site foundry.

Signature Hardware
2700 Crescent Springs Pike
Erlanger KY 41017
(+1) 866 855 2284
www.clawfootsupply.com

Complete supply of authentic reproduction clawfoot tubs, pedestal and console sinks, Topaz copper soaking tubs and more.

Stiffkey Bathrooms
89 Upper St Giles Street
Norwich
Norfolk NR2 1AB
+44 (0)1603 627850
www.stiffkeybathrooms.com

Antique sanitary ware and an individual range of period and bespoke bathroom accessories.

Vintage Plumbing
(+1) 818 772 1721
www.vintageplumbing.com

Original and restored to perfection bathroom antiques, including pull-chain toilets and clawfoot bathtubs.

The Water Monopoly
10–14 Lonsdale Road
London NW6 6RD
+44 (0)20 7624 2636
www.watermonopoly.com

Opulent period baths, basins and fittings.

BEDS

And So To Bed
0808 1444343
www.andsotobed.co.uk

The makers of Joanna Berryman's 'Handel' bed plus a huge range of beds in all styles and materials, from wooden sleigh beds to brass beds, mattresses, bedding and bedroom furnishings.

Bed Bazaar
The Old Station
Station Road
Framlingham
Suffolk IP13 9EE
+44 (0)1728 723756
www.bedbazaar.co.uk

Antique metal and wooden beds and hand made mattresses to order.

Natural Mat
Odhams Wharf
Topsham
Exeter EX3 0PD
+44 (0)1392 877247
www.naturalmat.co.uk

Organic mattresses made using entirely natural fibres, including lambswool, mohair, cashmere, cotton and bamboo.

BLINDS

Country Curtains
(+1) 800 937 1237
www.countrycurtains.com

Ready made Roman shades, roller shades and simple bamboo and wooden fibre shades.

Tidmarsh & Sons
Pleshey Lodge Farm
Pump Lane
Pleshey
Chelmsford
Essex CM3 1HF
+44 (0)1245 237228
www.tidmarsh.co.uk

All types of blind, including Venetian and Pinoleum blinds. Shutters are also available.

FABRICS

Annabel Grey Fabrics
The Old Barn
The Street
Corpustry
Norfolk NR11 6QP
+44 (0)1263 587781
www.annabelgrey.co.uk

Gorgeous, colourful designs with a vintage feel by textile designer and artist Annabel Grey.

Anta
Fearn
Tain
Ross-shire IV20 1XW
+44 (0)1862 832477
www.anta.co.uk

Plaids and checks in colours inspired by the Scottish landscape.

Bennison Fabrics
16 Holbein Place
London SW1W 8NL
+44 (0)20 7730 8076
www.bennisonfabrics.com

Tea-stained chintzes, faded florals, stripes and damasks for a look of faded elegance.

Cabbages & Roses
123 Sydney Street
London SW3 6NR
+44 (0)20 8487 2032
www.cabbagesandroses.com

Faded floral fabrics, bedding and cushions.

Chelsea Textiles
13 Walton Street
London SW3 2HX
+44 (0)20 7584 5544
www.chelseatextiles.com

Embroidered cottons, delicate prints, linens, silks and voiles with an 18th-century feel.

Colefax and Fowler
110 Fulham Road
London SW3 6HU
+44 (0)20 7244 7427
www.colefax.com

Quintessentially English fabrics and wallpapers.

Ian Mankin
271/273 Wandsworth Bridge Road
London SW6 2TX
+44 (0)20 7722 0997
www.ianmankin.co.uk

Natural fabrics, including linens, butter muslin and striped tickings.

Lewis & Wood
Woodchester Mill
North Woodchester
Stroud
Gloucestershire GL5 5NN
+44 (0)1453 878517
www.lewisandwood.co.uk

Gloriously eccentric wallpapers and fabrics.

Melin Tregwynt
Castlemorris
Haverfordwest
Pembrokeshire SA62 5UX
+44 (0)1348 891225
www.melintregwynt.co.uk

Cosy woven blankets, upholstery fabrics, throws and cushions.

Osborne & Little
+44 (0)20 7352 1456 (UK)
(+1) 203 359 1500 (US)
www.osborneandlittle.com

Traditional fabrics and trimmings to suit all tastes and styles of interior.

Russell & Chapple
68 Drury Lane
London WC2B 5SP
+44 (0)20 7836 7521
www.russellandchapple.com

Artist's canvas, jutes, fine muslin, deckchair canvas and hessian sacking.

St Jude's
+44 (0)1603 662951
www.stjudefabrics.co.uk

Artist-designed textiles with a vintage feel.

Tinsmiths

High Street
Ledbury
HR8 1DS
+44 (0)1531 632083
www.tinsmiths.co.uk

Lovely selection of tickings, stripes, cottons, and linens as well as a good range of simple lighting and attractive homewares.

ANTIQUE FABRICS

Beyond France

+44 (0)1285 641867
www.beyondfrance.co.uk

Large range of vintage linens, including monogrammed Hungarian grain and flour sacks and Romanian checked throws and tablecloths.

Katharine Pole

+44 (0)7747 616692
www.katharinepole.com

Wonderful selection of French textiles, including toiles, plain linens, and stripes.

Talent for Textiles

www.talentfortextiles.com

Talent for Textiles is a group of West Country antique dealers specializing in textiles who organize antique textiles fairs throughout the West Country, bringing together dealers in a series of attractive locations.

FENCING

John Waller

Bore Place
Chiddingstone
Edenbridge
Kent TN8 7AR
+44 (0)1892 740303
www.underwoodsman.co.uk

Recommended by Bella Pringle and Nick Ivins, for whom he wove chestnut garden fencing and a log basket.

FITTINGS

Clayton Munroe

+44 (0)1803 865700
www.claytonmunroe.com

Country style aged iron hinges and latches, available mail order only.

**Jim Lawrence
Traditional Ironwork**

+44 (0)1473 826685
www.jim-lawrence.co.uk

Ironwork with a hand-forged feel, from curtain poles and door handles to lighting and furniture.

Williamsburg Blacksmiths

26 Williams Street
Williamsburg, MA 01096
(+1) 800 248 1176
www.williamsburgblacksmiths.com

Authentic reproductions of traditional country and colonial designs.

FURNITURE – contemporary

Design Within Reach

www.dwr.com

Modern design, including mid-century classics such as the iconic Eames lounger and Bertoia chairs.

Pacha Design

+44 (0)1288 331505
www.pachadesign.co.uk

Furniture makers based in Cornwall and recommended by William Peers and Sophie Poklewski Koziell, for whom they made the oak sofa beds.

Pinch Design

+44 (0)20 7622 5075
www.pinchdesign.com

Elegant, and beautifully made wooden furniture

OKA

+44 (0)844 815 7380
www.okadirect.com

Good quality, mid-price furnishings in contemporary and traditional styles.

SCP

87 Westbourne Grove
London W2 4UL
+44 (0)20 7229 3612
www.scp.co.uk

Manufacturer and retailer of the work of contemporary British designers, including Matthew Hilton.

Whetstone Oak

+44 (0)1865 590507
www.whetstoneoak.co.uk

Made-to-order oak furniture.

FURNITURE – antique, vintage and traditional

Amy Perry Antiques

52 Long Street
Tetbury
Gloucestershire GL8 8AQ
+44 (0)1666 500354
www.amyperryantiques.co.uk

An off-beat collection of adaptable furniture.

Acorn Antiques

39 High Street
Dulverton
Somerset TA22 9DW
+44 (0)1398 323286
www.acornantiquesexmoor.co.uk

English antiques plus handmade Chesterfield, Knole and Howard sofas.

After Noah

121 Upper Street
Islington
London N1 1QP
+44 (0)207 3594281
www.afternoah.com

Antique, vintage, and contemporary furnishings.

Bright Lyons

383 Atlantic Avenue
Brooklyn, NY 11217
(+1) 718 855 5463
www.brightlyons.com

Vintage mid-century furniture and the source of Sam Denny-Hodson and Paul Vogel's Eames lounger (see pages 170–171). Will ship to UK.

Collingwood Cotehele Design

High Street
Yoxford
Saxmundham
Suffolk IP17 3EP
+44 (0)1728 668997
www.collingwoodcoteheledesign.co.uk

Interior design company also stocking furniture and antiques.

English Country Antiques

26 Snake Hollow Road
P. O. Box 1995
Bridgehampton, NY 11932
(+1) 631 537 0606
www.ecantiques.com

Antiques and accessories.

Fiske & Freeman

32 South Main Street
Ipswich, MA
(+1) 978 356 3861
www.fiskeandfreeman.com

English country antiques.

George Smith

587–589 Kings Road
London SW6 2EH
+44 (0)20 7384 1004
www.georgesmith.com

Traditional sofas and armchairs.

Joanna Booth Antiques

+44 (0)20 7352 8998 for an appointment
www.joannabooth.co.uk

Early and rare antiques including sculpture and tapestries.

James Petre

+44 (0)7890 262247
www.quirkyinteriors.co.uk

Based in Hertfordshire, this design workshop has developed its own variety of reclaimed furniture and other items, including fruit-box tables and zinc-topped chests.

Josephine Ryan Antiques

www.josephineryanantiques.co.uk

An antiques dealer with her finger on the fashion pulse.

Leigh Extence

+44 (0)1395 268723
www.extence.co.uk

Antique clocks including that English essential, the grandfather clock.

Lloyd Loom

+44 (0)1277 812777
www.lloyd-loom-furniture.co.uk

New versions of the ubiquitous and loveable furnishings made from twisted paper and wire.

Margaret Howell

34 Wigmore Street
London W1U 2RS
+44 (0)20 7009 9009
www.margarethowell.co.uk

Twentieth-century British design classics, from Ercol to Anglepoise, to match the pared-down aesthetic of the clothes.

The Odd Chair Company

www.theoddchaircompany.com

Traditional and unusual chairs, both antique and reproduction.

Restoration Hardware

(+1) 800 910 9836
www.restorationhardware.com

Updated classics and reproductions, including farmhouse tables made from reclaimed British pine.

FURNITURE RESTORATION

Fiona Valentine

+44 (0)1456 383632
(recommended by Ursula Falconer)

FLOORING

Alternative Flooring Company

+44 (0)1264 335111
www.alternativeflooring.com

Coir, sea-grass, sisal, jute and wool floor coverings.

Bernard Dru Oak

+44 (0)1643 841312
www.oakfloor.co.uk

Specialists in oak flooring.

Crucial Trading

+44 (0)1562 743747
www.crucial-trading.com

Natural floorings, most of which can also be ordered as rugs bound with cotton, linen or leather.

The Delabole Slate Company

Pengelly
Delabole
Cornwall PL33 9AZ
+44 (0)1840 212242
www.delaboleslate.co.uk

Riven slate or slate slabs suitable for work surfaces, fireplaces and flooring.

Roger Oates Design

1 Munro Terrace
London SW10 0DL
+44 (0)20 73512288
www.rogeroates.com

All types of natural floorings plus flat-weave rugs and runners.

Rush Matters

+44 (0)1234 376419
www.rushmatters.co.uk

Rush matting made with English rushes, also baskets and rush seating for chairs.

The Natural Wood Floor Company

20 Smugglers Way
Wandsworth
London SW18 1EQ
+44 (0)20 8871 9771
www.naturalwoodfloor.co.uk

Solid and parquet woodblock flooring.

Victorian Woodworks

158 Walton Street
London SW3 2JL
+44 (0)20 8534 1000

www.victorianwoodworks.co.uk

Reclaimed, new and
antique timber flooring
and joinery.

HEATING

Bisque

244 Belsize Road
London NW6 4BT
+44 (0)20 7328 2225

www.bisque.co.uk

Suppliers of classic
radiators.

Chesneys

194–202 Battersea
Park Road
London SW11 4ND
+44 (0)20 7627 1410

www.chesneys.co.uk

Huge range of modern
and antique fireplaces.

The Windy Smithy

Bishops Plot
Blackborough
Cullompton
Devon EX15 2HY
+44 (0)7866 241783

www.windysmithy.co.uk

Blacksmith and tool maker
who specializes in bespoke
woodburning stoves.

FINISHING TOUCHES

Abigail Ahern

137 Upper Street
London N1 1QP
+44 (0)20 7354 8181

www.abigailahern.com

Eccentric and unusual
furniture, wallpaper,
lighting and ceramics.

Anthropologie

Visit the website for a list
of stores across North
America and the UK

www.anthropologie.com

Vintage-inspired and
one-of-a-kind decorative
details and tableware.

Graham & Green

4 Elgin Crescent
London W11 2HX
+44 (0)20 7243 8908
+44 (0)1225 418 200 for mail
order and customer service

www.grahamandgreen.co.uk

Glamorous and quirky
glass, cushions, tableware,
lighting and a small range
of furniture.

Labour and Wait

85 Redchurch Street
London E2 7DJ
+44 (0)20 7729 6253

www.labourandwait.co.uk

Functional and beautiful
homewares, both new
and vintage, including
kitchen enamelware
and zinc buckets.

Lush Designs

8 College Approach
Greenwich
London SE10 9HY
+44 (0)20 8293 5662

www.lushlampshades.co.uk

Bold, beautifully drawn
patterns featuring animals
and plants on lampshades,
cushions, tea towels and
more, with a distinctly
English, slightly primitive
charm.

Made in Cley

High Street
Cley-next-the-sea
Nr. Holt
Norfolk NR25 7RF
+44 (0)1263 740134

www.madeincley.co.uk

Locally made ceramics,
including porcelain,
earthenware and raku.

Papa Stour

+44 (0)7922 771412

www.papastour.com

Online Scottish design from
cushions to deerskins.

Townhouse Spitalfields

5 Fournier Street
London E1 6QE
+44 (0)20 7247 4745

www.townhousespitalfields.com

Irresistible mix of antique
and contemporary
furnishings, ceramics, and
textiles, and 20th-century
British art all displayed in
the setting of a beautiful,
early 18th-century house.

JOINERY

Peter Bennett

+44 (0)1404 831403

www.pbw.co.uk

Joiner who built the
cupboards in Maddie's
house (see pages 140–147).

KITCHENS

Aga Rayburn

+44 (0)8457 125207

www.agaliving.com

Classic cast-iron range
cookers, essential for the
country kitchen.

Barnes of Ashburton

24A West Street
Ashburton
Newton Abbot
Devon TQ13 7DU
+44 (0)1364 653613

www.barnesofashburton.co.uk

Elegant bespoke
kitchens and handmade
freestanding units and
furniture.

Crabtree Kitchens

Finewood Interiors
Blacknest House
Blacknest Business Park
Bentley
Hampshire GU34 4PX
+44 (0)1420 23883

www.crabtreekitchens.co.uk

Traditional kitchens.

Crown Point Cabinetry

153 Charlestown Road
Claremont, NH 03743
(+1) 800 999 4994

www.crown-point.com

Custom cabinets for
kitchen and bath.

Fired Earth

117–119 Fulham Road
London SW3 6RL
+44 (0)7589 0489

www.firedearth.com

Kitchens, bathrooms,
and tiles with a traditional
handcrafted feel, also an
excellent range of paint
colours.

Harrington Brassworks

(+1) 201 818 1300

www.harringtonbrassworks.com

Brass faucets for kitchen
and bath in classic styles.

Plain English

28 Blandford Street
London W1U 4BZ
+44 (0)20 7486 2674
and at
Stowupland Hall
Stowupland
Stowmarket
Suffolk IP14 4BE
+44 (0)1449 774028

www.plainenglishdesign.co.uk

Elegant, simple and classic
wooden kitchens.

PAINT

Benjamin Moore

(+1) 855-724-6802 for
stockists and advice

www.benjaminmoore.com

High quality paints and
stains in a rainbow of
shades. Producers of the
Colonial Williamsburg
historic colour palette.

Farrow & Ball

+44 (0)1202 876141

www.farrow-ball.com

Subtle paint colours
with strange names;
also papers, varnishes
and stains.

Francesca's Paints

34 Battersea Business
Centre
99/109 Lavender Hill
London SW11 5QL
+44 (0)20 7228 7694

www.francescaspaint.com

Traditional limewash,
eco emulsion paint and
chalky emulsion.

Janovic

(+1) 800 772 4381

www.janovic.com

Quality paints from a
wide variety of makers.

Paint & Paper Library

5 Elystan Street
London SW3 3NT
+44 (0)20 7590 9860

www.paintlibrary.co.uk

Excellent quality paint
and wallpaper.

Papers and Paints

4 Park Walk
London SW10 0AD
+44 (0)20 7352 8626

www.papers-paints.co.uk

In addition to their own
range of paints, this
company will mix any
colour to order.

Rose of Jericho

+44 (0)1935 83676

www.rose-of-jericho.demon.co.uk

Hand-made limewashes,
distempers, flat oils,
emulsions and eggshell
paints. Also lime, mortars
and plasters. All products
are designed especially for
the sensitive decoration of
traditional and historic
buildings.

LIGHTING

Eron Johnson Antiques

451 North Broadway
Denver, CO 80203
(+1) 303 777 8700

www.eronjohnsonantiques.com

Antique table lamps,
wall sconces and
brass candelabra and
candlesticks, as well as
architectural salvage, fine
furniture and decorative
accessories.

John Cullen

561–563 Kings Road
London SW6 2EB
+44 (0)20 7371 5400

www.johncullenlighting.co.uk

Extensive range of
contemporary light fittings
and a bespoke lighting
design service.

Vaughan Ltd.

G1, Chelsea Harbour
Design Centre
Chelsea Harbour
London SW10 0XE
+44 (0)20 7349 4600

www.vaughandesigns.com

Comprehensive range
of replica period lighting
from lamps to sconces
to chandeliers.

PLASTERWORK

Tom Verity

+44 (0)7932 752957
(recommended by
Ursula Falconer)

PORTRAITS

Maggie Hadfield's daughter,
Kate Blunt, paints portraits
to commission.
+44 (0)7748 300836

WALLCOVERINGS

Colefax & Fowler
(see under fabrics)

Lewis & Wood
(see under Fabrics)

Architects, Artists, Designers and Business Owners whose work has been featured in this book:

Joanna Berryman

+44 (0)20 7209 5826

www.joberryman.com

Pages 176–183, 184 centre,
185 above right, 185 below left.

Andrew Blackman Ltd

www.andrewblackman.com

Specialist dealer in
Old Master paintings.

Pages 38–39, 70–79.

**Kate Blunt
Portrait painter**

+44 (0)7748 300836

Pages 40–49, 192.

Hein Bonger

22 High Street
Saxmundham
Suffolk IP17 1AJ

Source of many of the
paintings and furniture
in Alison Hill's house.

Pages 71, 122–123, 148–155,
156 centre, 156 below.

Botelet Farm

Herodsfoot
Liskeard
Cornwall PL14 4RD
+44 (0)1503 220 225

www.botelet.com

Organic B&B and
meadow camping plus two
self-catering cottages and
two yurts available for holiday
accommodation. Design by
Richard Tamblyn.

Pages 22–29, 36 centre.

Mark Brazier-Jones

Hyde Hall Barn
Buckland
Sandon
Buntingford
Hertfordshire SG9 0RU
+44 (0)1763 273599

www.brazier-jones.com

Pages 160–167, 184 above, 184 below,
185 above left.

Becca and Bill Collison

www.bills-website.co.uk

Bill's Restaurants can
be found nationwide.

Pages 92–99, 121 above left,
121 below right.

**Becca and Bill's kitchen
made by:**

Woodworks of Lewes
Bespoke English Kitchens
1 Malling Street
Lewes
East Sussex BN7 2RA
(+44) 01273 471269

www.woodworkslewes.com

Page 93 left.

**Toby Falconer (architect) at
John Falconer Associates**

101 Promenade
Cheltenham
Gloucestershire GL50 1NW
+44 (0)1242 582362

Paintings by Peter Lloyd-Jones,
wallpaper in hall by Lewis &
Wood, chair fabric by Vanessa
Arbuthnott.

Pages 4–5, 110–119, 120 centre, 120 below,
121 below left.

**Matt Fothergill
Leather Designs & Production**

17 Bull Ring
Ludlow
SY8 1AD
+44 (0)1584 876210

www.mattfothergill.com

Pages 30–35, 36 above, 37 above left,
37 below left.

Bella and Nick Ivins

www.wildweddings.co.uk

Wild Weddings is Nick and
Bella's documentary wedding
photography company. They
are also the authors of *The New
Homesteader*, a book about
their life at Walnuts Farm.

Pages 2, 7 centre, 132–139, 156 above,
157 above.

**Eva Johnson
Trip Trap Scandinavian
Woodcare Products:**

www.evajohnson.com
www.evajohnson.co.uk

Pages 8, 124–131, 157 below.

**Holly Keeling
Interior stylist**

Heathfield Farm
Denbury
Newton Abbot
Devon TQ12 6ES
+44 (0)7835 100577

www.hollykeeling.co.uk

Pages 1, 7 right, 80–91, 120 above,
121 above right.

**Holly Keeling's kitchen
(designed by Holly Keeling)
made by:**

Barnes of Ashburton
24a West Street
Ashburton
Newton Abbot
Devon TQ13 7DU
+44 (0)1364 653613

www.barnesofashburton.co.uk

Pages 84 below, 85.

Patricia Low

Patricia Low's pots
can be seen at:

The Fine Art Society
148 New Bond Street
London W1S 2JT
+44 (0)20 7629 5116

www.faslondon.com

and by appointment
at "Tidpit Works!"

E: 1000@btinternet.com

Pages 3, 100–109.

Lori and William Gibson

Interior design by
**Guy Oliver at
Oliver Laws Ltd**

47 Conduit Street
London W1S 2YP
+44 (0)20 7437 8487

www.oliverlaws.com

Pages 50–57.

**William Peers and Sophie
Poklewski Koziell**

www.williampeers.com

William Peers is available
to commission as a sculptor.

Pages 9–21, 36 below, 37 right.

Richard Smith

www.madeaux.com

and

No. 9 by Jim Thompson

www.jimthompsonfabrics.com

Hand-printed fabrics
and wallpapers.

Pages 38–39, 70–79.

**Doris Urquhart and
Christopher Richardson**

York's Tenement
Darsham Road
Yoxford
Suffolk IP17 3LA
+44 (0)1728 668038

www.aayt.co.uk

Antique shop and barn
available for holiday
accommodation.

Pages 6, 58–69.

Plants from

Darsham Nurseries

www.darshamnurseries.co.uk

**Paul Vogel and Sam
Denny-Hodson**

Packway Farm
Halesworth Road
Chediston
Halesworth
Suffolk IP19 0AE
+44 (0)1986 785 550

www.paulvogel.com
www.paulvogelbedlinen.com

Stylish holiday cottages
available for holiday
accommodation.

Pages 158–159, 168–175, 185 above
centre; 185 below right.

Picture Credits

All photography by Jan Baldwin.

1 The family home of stylist Holly Keeling www.hollykeeling.co.uk; 2 Nick and Bella Ivins, www.walnutsfarm.co.uk; 3 The home of the ceramicist Patricia Low in Hampshire; 4–5 The family home of Ursula and Toby Falconer; 6 The home of Doris Urquhart and Christopher Richardson, antiques dealers in Suffolk; 7 left Alison Hill and John Taylor's home in Suffolk; 7 centre Nick and Bella Ivins, www.walnutsfarm.co.uk; 7 right The family home of stylist Holly Keeling www.hollykeeling.co.uk; 8 The home of Eva Johnson in Suffolk; 9–21 William Peers and Sophie Poklewski Koziell; 22–29 Botelet Farm, a special place to stay in Cornwall www.botelet.com; 30–35 & 36 above The home of Matt and Jax Fothergill in Shropshire; 36 centre Botelet Farm, a special place to stay in Cornwall www.botelet.com; 36 below William Peers and Sophie Poklewski Koziell; 37 The home of Matt and Jax Fothergill in Shropshire; 37 right William Peers and Sophie Poklewski Koziell; 38–39 The home of textile designer Richard Smith and art dealer Andrew Blackman; 50–57 The home of Lori and William Gibson; 58–69 The home of Doris Urquhart and Christopher Richardson, antiques dealers in Suffolk; 70–79 The home of textile designer Richard Smith and art dealer Andrew Blackman; 80–91 The family home of stylist Holly Keeling www.hollykeeling.co.uk; 92–99 The family home of Becca and Bill Collison in Sussex; 100–109 The home of the ceramicist Patricia Low in Hampshire; 110–119 The family home of Ursula and Toby Falconer; 120 above The family home of stylist Holly Keeling www.hollykeeling.co.uk; 120 centre & below The family home of Ursula and Toby Falconer; 121 above left The family home of Becca and Bill Collison in Sussex; 121 above right The family home of stylist Holly Keeling www.hollykeeling.co.uk; 121 below left The family home of Ursula and Toby Falconer; 121 below right The family home of Becca and Bill Collison in Sussex; 122–123 Alison Hill and John Taylor's home in Suffolk; 124–131 The home of Eva Johnson in Suffolk; 132–139 Nick and Bella Ivins, www.walnutsfarm.co.uk; 148–155 Alison Hill and John Taylor's home in Suffolk; 156 above Nick and Bella Ivins, www.walnutsfarm.co.uk; 156 centre & below Alison Hill and John Taylor's home in Suffolk; 157 above Nick and Bella Ivins, www.walnutsfarm.co.uk; 157 below The home of Eva Johnson in Suffolk; 158–159 The home of textile designer Paul Vogel and his wife Sam Denny-Hodson; 160–167 the Hertfordshire home of Mark Brazier-Jones, creator of bespoke furniture, lighting and functional art. www.Brazier-Jones.com; 168–175 The home of textile designer Paul Vogel and his wife Sam Denny-Hodson; 176–183 'The Folly' designed by Joanna Berryman. For interior design commissions please contact Joanna at Matrushka.co.uk; 184 above & below the Hertfordshire home of Mark Brazier-Jones, creator of bespoke furniture, lighting and functional art, www.Brazier-Jones.com; 184 centre 'The Folly' designed by Joanna Berryman. For interior design commissions please contact Joanna at Matrushka.co.uk; 185 above left Hertfordshire home of Mark Brazier-Jones, creator of bespoke furniture, lighting and functional art www.Brazier-Jones.com; 185 above centre The home of textile designer Paul Vogel and his wife Sam Denny-Hodson; 185 above right and below left 'The Folly' designed by Joanna Berryman. For interior design commissions please contact Joanna at Matrushka.co.uk; 185 below right The home of textile designer Paul Vogel and his wife Sam Denny-Hodson.

INDEX

Figures in italics indicate captions.

ACKNOWLEDGMENTS

This book has been a particular pleasure to write, partly because I have met such interesting people while visiting some very beautiful parts of England, but also because I have so enjoyed working with Jan Baldwin, her assistants Peter Dixon, Wayne Kirk and Helen Carter, and with the team at Ryland Peters & Small. Jan's superb photographs speak for themselves; less visible is the hard work and enterprise of Jess Walton, whose connections, eye and knowledge as a location researcher were invaluable. Annabel Morgan is the most supportive editor a writer could wish for, and designer Paul Tilby has fitted text and photographs together with patience and flexibility, as well as creativity. Thanks are also due to Art Director Leslie Harrington, Publishing Director Cindy Richards and Publicity Manager Lauren Wright, and to Emily Westlake for additional help with locations. My father, George Byam Shaw, again trawled his prodigious literary memory for poetical quotations, and my daughter Lydia did an excellent job with the stockists' list. Miranda Eden came up with a wonderful location from her enviable address book, and all the house owners were, without exception, hospitable and kind. Lastly, I am indebted to Alison Starling, whose idea it was to write about farmhouses.